Debra Fileta writes with ................................................ She
shows all of us how to overcome the inevitable challenges of married life by
making the right choices. In short, Debra reveals how choosing marriage,
every day, leads to deep and abiding lifelong love. Whether you are single,
engaged, or married, you don't want to miss out on this profound and practical message.

—Drs. Les and Leslie Parrott, *New York Times* bestselling authors of
*Saving Your Marriage Before It Starts*

No matter what season of marriage you are in, *Choosing Marriage* will offer
encouragement and hope to find even more satisfaction in your relationship.
Debra's counseling experience and biblical knowledge are woven together
with some great stories and practical advice to help every couple learn how
to experience a richer, more meaningful life together.

—John Fuller, Focus on the Family

*Choosing Marriage* is the kind of book that you will underline, highlight,
dog-ear, reread, and then subtly leave open on your spouse's side of the bed
for them to (hopefully) pick up and read, forcing you to purchase clean copies for your family and friends. When we were seeking an author/speaker/
expert for a large event on marriage and relationships in California, we
chose Debra Fileta, and the attenders loved her. When college students and
young adults seek dating and relationship advice, we gift them with a copy
of *True Love Dates*. And now, whenever we counsel those seeking insight
and advice on marriage, we plan to give them *Choosing Marriage*. It is an
engaging, insightful, and professional look into the most intimate of all of
our relationships—our marriages—that is based on Debra's clinical expertise, sound research, and her own personal journey. For those of you who
seek to choose marriage—who desire authentic intimacy, biblical insights,
and practical ways to grow your marriage—you are holding the best book
you can find in your hands. Please wait to highlight or dog-ear it until after
you purchase it.

—Dr. Chris and Alisa Grace, Center for Marriage and Relationships,
Biola University

When I met Debra Fileta, I was instantly encouraged—and you will be too. Whether you're a happy couple, a couple in need of help, or a single looking ahead, *Choosing Marriage* is a tour de force for anyone seeking to achieve a great marriage. My team and I see a lot of great marriage books—and this is one of the best we've ever read. You'll quickly find practical, achievable suggestions, humor, and road-tested insight from years of working marriage therapy. Debra's focus on believing the best echoes my own research into happy marriages, and her advice for couples in need provides hope for those who need it most. This is a must-read!

—Shaunti Feldhahn, social researcher and bestselling author of
*For Women Only* and *The Surprising Secrets of Highly Happy Marriages*

Put this book at the top of your reading list and buy one for a friend! My bride and I really enjoyed reading *Choosing Marriage* together. We were inspired and challenged to have a healthier relationship and given practical advice on how to do it. It's evident that Debra is not only a much-sought-after national speaker but also a highly skilled author.

—Chris Reed, pastor to 20s/30s and singles at Saddleback Church,
Lake Forest, California

Debra Fileta is a gifted counselor and an excellent communicator. *Choosing Marriage* is a true masterpiece among the crowded shelves of marriage books. It is for everyone who is married or has a future marriage on their radar. Debra very practically walks you through changes that will literally transform any marriage. *Choosing Marriage* redefines real hope in marriage!

—Kim Kimberling, founder of Awesome Marriage and author of
*7 Secrets to an Awesome Marriage*

*Choosing Marriage* is a must-read for anyone who is hoping to marry someday and for those who want to improve their marriage. Debra Fileta masterfully addresses what it takes to cultivate and keep a thriving marriage through real life stories, practical tips, Scripture, and probing questions. She gives both married and single people hope that they too can foster an amazing, lifelong marriage with the one they love.

—Dave and Ashley Willis, StrongerMarriages.org

DEBRA FILETA, M.A., LPC

# Choosing Marriage

HARVEST HOUSE PUBLISHERS
EUGENE, OREGON

Cover by Emily Weigel

Cover photos © Doczky / Shutterstock ; sagesmaskelemen / creativemarket.com

Published in association with the literary agency of D.C. Jacobson & Associates LLC, an author management company. www.dcjacobson.com

The names and identifying information of the people discussed in this book have been changed to protect their identities and to respect their confidentiality. Where individuals may be identifiable, they have granted the author and publisher the right to use their name, stories, and/or facts of their lives in all manners.

## Choosing Marriage

Copyright © 2018 by Debra Fileta

Published by Harvest House Publishers
Eugene, Oregon 97408
www.harvesthousepublishers.com

ISBN 978-0-7369-7338-0 (pbk.)
ISBN 978-0-7369-7339-7 (eBook)

Library of Congress Cataloging-in-Publication Data

Names: Fileta, Debra K., author.
Title: Choosing marriage / Debra Fileta.
Description: Eugene, Oregon : Harvest House Publishers, 2018. | Includes
   bibliographical references and index.
Identifiers: LCCN 2018002888 (print) | LCCN 2017049635 (ebook) | ISBN
   9780736973397 (ebook) | ISBN 9780736973380 (pbk. : alk. paper)
Subjects: LCSH: Marriage—Religious aspects—Christianity.
Classification: LCC BV835 (print) | LCC BV835 .F543 2018 (ebook) | DDC
   248.8/44—dc23
LC record available at https://lccn.loc.gov/2018002888

**Printed in the United States of America**

18 19 20 21 22 23 24 25 26 / BP-SK / 10 9 8 7 6 5 4 3 2 1

*To my sweet husband, John*
*Your love, devotion, dedication, and commitment to me*
*and to our marriage are evident in everything you do.*
*Thank you for inspiring these pages.*

*To Ella, Eli, and Ezra*
*The three of you have given me a deeper*
*understanding of love and an overflowing joy.*
*May God continue leading your precious hearts toward Him.*

# Contents

# Foreword

Because of a degenerative eye disease, I live with basically one eye. You wouldn't know it looking at me, but an ophthalmologist explained to me that my left eye has reached the point where my brain doesn't rely on it anymore. What I see comes largely through my right eye.

I write with "one eye" too. I'm a "spiritual" writer, steeped in the Christian classics, theology, and decades of studying Scripture. When I address marriage, it's automatic for me to view it through that one lens.

Debra Fileta writes with two eyes. She has an uncanny "spiritual" awareness. By that I mean she understands not just biblical *truth*, but also biblical *sense*. Added to that, however, her other "eye" is the eye of a trained marriage therapist. She has worked successfully with numerous couples and can see patterns that "thinkers" who often write in book-paneled rooms might miss.

Take just the title of this book, for instance. *Choosing Marriage* is a marvelous way to describe, in just two words, the spirituality of marital commitment. It is loaded with profound theological meaning and provides a helpful metaphor. But Debra doesn't stop there.

She offers numerous tools to make choosing marriage seem possible and practical.

In other words, Debra doesn't just *inspire* us—plenty of "spiritual" writers do that; she also *equips* us. Rare is the writer who lives in both worlds so effectively.

You are about to enter the world of a humble wife who freely admits her own mistakes; a delightful companion who is enjoyable to spend time with; a partner in a marriage who inspires, amuses, and encourages; and a therapist who knows how to get your marriage from point A to point B.

Pour yourself a cup of tea, take time between chapters to savor the truth, and remind yourself why you got married—or want to be married. With Debra's gentle coaching, be equipped to keep choosing marriage.

Gary Thomas
Author of *Sacred Marriage*
September 2017

# A Note from the Author

Dear Friend,
    I am so thankful you've picked up this book. I've thought of you and I've prayed for you as I typed each page and thought through each chapter. I don't know your name, and I may not know your specific story, but one thing I do know is that we're on this journey of life together, in need of God and in need of one another along the way. It has been said that "we read to know we are not alone."[1] My prayer is that through these pages, you will know you are not alone and be encouraged to continue moving in the direction of healing and hope.

## This Book Is For...

*Married couples:* This book is written for married couples who are facing—or may one day face—the routine hardships and struggles that come with marriage. It's a book for couples who are either filled with hope or low on hope, offering them practical steps to take themselves and their marriages to a better place. It will encourage, inspire, and equip them to see that choosing marriage is not just a one-time decision, but a choice we must learn to make every single day.

*Engaged Couples:* This book is also for those who are anticipating entering marriage. Too many couples are going into marriage unprepared for this significant life change and the challenges they will face. I believe with all my heart that the more you know before marriage, the better you'll do in marriage. This book will prepare and equip engaged couples, empowering them as they look forward to the commitment of choosing marriage.

*Singles:* When it comes to learning about marriage and healthy relationships, you can never start too early. In fact, I believe the greatest times of learning and preparation for marriage happen while you're standing alone. This book is for any single person who is hoping to get a front-row seat to the ingredients of creating a healthy marriage. Often our culture paints a negative view of marriage, questioning if a good marriage is even possible. This book will encourage and inspire you to see that choosing marriage is certainly worth the work.

## This Book Is Not For...

As a licensed professional counselor, I know some of you picking up this book come from a background with issues of abuse, addiction, or abandonment that trump the routine hardships and struggles of marriage. You feel discouraged, alone, and hopeless, and you're desperate for something to make your marriage better. If this is you, know that while the concepts in this book may offer you encouragement in your healing process, the journey of healing is not one you should ever be walking alone. You need to understand many important principles and practices for dealing with abuse, addiction, and abandonment, and your *highest priorities* should be your own physical safety, emotional well-being, and spiritual nourishment. It's important to seek the help of a professional counselor to help you navigate your specific journey of healing, starting by getting healthy from the inside out.

Whoever you are and wherever you are on this journey, I'm so thankful that you've entrusted me to be a part of it. I look forward to praying for you and hearing from you along the way.

Sincerely,

*Debra*

# Choosing Marriage

*The Hardest and Greatest Thing*

Did you ever think someone could show you love through a bologna sandwich? I didn't think so either. Until I found out my then boyfriend (now husband)—a broke medical student at the time—spent close to two months eating bologna sandwiches every day to cut down his grocery budget to ten dollars per week, just so he could save enough money to buy me an engagement ring.

Marriage will cost you. In big ways and in small ways.

When you think of the cost of marriage, what comes to mind? According to recent statistics, couples today spend an average of $26,720 on a wedding.[1] That's a lot of money, but it's nothing compared to the cost of marriage. Marriage will cost you more. It will cost you something great. It will cost you a price much higher than the money you spend on a ring, or a wedding, or a cake, or a honeymoon. It will cost you yourself.

## The Real Cost

Too often people enter marriage with high expectations coupled with low awareness of what it involves. While most people entering marriage have heard the phrase "marriage requires sacrifice," they have no idea what that sacrifice will entail. In a recent survey I took of over 1000 singles, three quarters of them agreed with the statement that *marriage will require sacrifice*, yet close to half of them believed marriage would also be "easy." I don't know about you, but I'm fairly certain the words *sacrifice* and *easy* don't go hand in hand.

"I don't get it. This was supposed to be simple. I thought that once the wedding bells rang, we'd be 'happily ever after.'" I was counseling a young woman who found herself trying to reconcile the differences between her expectations of marriage and the reality of marriage. And she's certainly not alone in this disconnect. So many people think happily ever after just happens along the way.

Oftentimes we don't have the hard conversations before marriage, and many important topics—from sexual expectations to financial habits to family history—tend to get pushed to the back burner as we're prepping for the wedding. We're more concerned about the flavor of our wedding cake than about how we'll manage conflict and communication. We're so busy creating the perfect wedding announcement that we fail to discuss creating the best atmosphere for our future marriage. It's almost as though we're ashamed to admit that the process of becoming one might be difficult! Maybe we think discussing our apprehensions will make us look weak, or sinful, or selfish, and so we pretend the hard things don't exist. And for those of us who attempt to have the important conversations, those conversations tend to be incomplete.

When I surveyed more than 1000 married men and women, more than 96 percent of them said they believe the average person does *not* understand the cost of marriage going into it. That's a staggering number. It tells me we're given the blanket statement that "marriage will be hard," but we're not really prepared to tackle those hardships when they come. We're not trained. We're not equipped. We're not even aware. We don't know what to look for. We assume that two good people trying to do the right thing will always equal a good, strong marriage. But unfortunately, as I've seen time and time again in my counseling office, that's simply not the case.

Even though marriage is one of the most significant choices you will make in life, it's the only one you're given a license to do before you've actually learned how to do it! Every other major, licensed accomplishment comes by way of a substantial amount of time, energy, education, and preparation. You go through eight strenuous years of training to get a medical license. You have to clock numerous hours of driving to get a driver's license. But marriage? For marriage you get a license *first* and hope you somehow learn to succeed along the way. Is it just me, or does that sound a little backward?

Just like anything worthwhile, marriage requires knowledge, training, effort, and sacrifice. It requires daily choices—sometimes big, mostly small, and often hard—that lead to a lifetime of love and a fulfilling marriage. But if you're not prepared to make those choices, you can end up making the wrong decision every single time.

## Marriage Is Not About You

I sat down on my comfortable gray sofa, grabbed my fuzzy blanket, stretched out my legs, and turned on the TV to relax after a long day. Then I heard it.

"I shouldn't be with someone if I'm not happy."

My stomach turned. I was watching *Married at First Sight*, a reality show that portrays the ultimate dating game. Now, reality television isn't my typical cup of tea—I'd rather spend my evening watching a good documentary than overdosing on drama. But something about this program piqued my interest. In the show, psychologists and relationship experts conduct a battery of psychological tests and interviews with a group of men and women, ultimately matching two candidates. They meet for the first time at the altar.

The legally married couple is then followed around by camera crews as they navigate the ups and downs of the first two months of marriage. At the end of the eight weeks, they're given the option of staying together or getting divorced (which in and of itself shows you the commitment level we're talking about here if eight weeks is all it takes to choose divorce).

While I absolutely disagreed with a lot of things about this show, what intrigued me the most were the high expectations and grand assumptions the candidates had about marriage, inevitably followed by the hardships that come when their dreams of marriage are faced with the realities of marriage. They go into marriage with the goal of what marriage will do for them, rather than what they will do for their marriage.

What an accurate reflection of the self-centered society we live in, falsely believing that the main goal of life is our own personal happiness. If you're getting married with this as your goal—to make yourself happy—you will be disappointed in a severe way. There will be a moment, a day, or even a season in marriage when, like it or not, you won't be happy. That's the nature of a relationship where two flawed people are rubbing up against each other daily. There's bound to be a moment when someone is not happy!

But marriage is not simply about your happiness. It's not even about you. It's about unconditional love, which we choose to give time and time again. It's about sacrificing, serving, giving, and forgiving, and then doing it over again. No wonder it's so much easier to choose divorce over marriage at the end of an eight-week reality show marriage, and often at the end of a real marriage. When the cost of marriage becomes too great, we convince ourselves we have nothing left to gain, and therefore nothing left to give.

It could be after a silly argument.

It could be a heated moment, when words have been said that can't be taken back.

It could be in the middle of a misunderstanding.

It could be in an instant when trust has been broken.

It could be a time when your needs have not been understood.

But no matter what it is, there will be a moment when you are given the option of two choices: self or marriage. *Me* or *we*. And in every single moment like this, a choice will have to be made.

## Why Choose Marriage?

We live in a culture that is currently questioning the very foundation of marriage, from both within the church and without. According to recent surveys, many millennials are on the verge of believing that marriage is a lost art, rebelling against the idea of a permanent, lifelong relationship with another human being.[2] They wonder, *Can I even handle marriage?* Popular relationship columnist Anthony D'Ambrosio answers that question with a no, claiming "marriages today just don't work."[3] He blames this generation's lack of ability to handle marriage on five things: poor sex lives, financial burdens, social media, emotional disconnects, and unhealthy desires for attention. While acknowledging defeat in his own marriage, he justifies himself by saying, "The world has put roadblocks in the way of getting there and living a happy life with someone. Some things are in our control, and unfortunately, others are not."[4]

While I absolutely agree that everything he mentioned plays a significant role in attacking marriages today (and *all* relationships), the author forgot one crucial element: God. We have everything we need to overcome life's obstacles because we were *made* for love by a God who made us in His image. We were *made* for commitment by a God who entered covenant with us. We were created to do this thing called marriage, and created to do it well.

My heart breaks for the men and women who are questioning marriage, whether from within or from without, because I believe their sincere questioning ultimately stems from significant wounds, major hurts, and deep disappointments. While marriage may be hard, the loss of a marriage is even harder. I know, because in addition to observing people dealing with divorce in my professional career, I have witnessed people very close to me walk through the devastating pain of divorce. Nothing breaks hearts and turns worlds upside down more than the loss of this kind of love. Why else do you think God "hates" divorce (Malachi 2:16 NLT)? It's certainly not because He's a legalistic, angry God who wants us to stick to the rules. According to this verse of Scripture, it's not simply about divorce but about the devastation it causes in its aftermath. God hates divorce because He knows the excruciating pain it causes in the hearts and lives of His children.

*interesting*

Even with the claims that this generation "cannot handle marriage," I for one am not about to throw in the towel on the concept of choosing marriage—for both married couples and singles alike. I'm not going to lie or pretend marriage is always an easy road, because it's not. But nothing worthwhile in life comes easy. I tell the marriage and premarriage couples I counsel that at some point we all want out because we're human, and there's no one human being on earth who will give us everything we need. Marriage is work, but working on your marriage is the best work you will ever do. Let me tell you why.

*Because marriage makes you better.* When we go into marriage with the idea that it is meant only for our happiness, we will be disappointed every single time we're not happy. No human being on earth can bring eternal joy into our lives, because they weren't made to have that role. Real marriage is not about being happy and fulfilled for the rest of our lives; it's about the two of us becoming the best we can be from this day forward. Proverbs 27:17 teaches that "as iron sharpens iron, so one person sharpens another."

*only God can.*

In his book *Sacred Marriage*, author Gary Thomas challenges men and women to realize that marriage isn't just about happiness; it's about *holiness.* Through the un-replicated commitment and intimacy of marriage, we have the opportunity for lifelong growth and maturity, practicing selflessness, forgiveness, and grace as we learn to love each other unconditionally. Two imperfect human beings exposing their realness, yet loving each other still.

But harder yet for some, marriage makes us better because we learn to *receive* that kind of love for ourselves. For us to truly become better, we must learn to receive love as readily as we give it. One of my favorite passages in the Bible encourages us to love our neighbor as we love ourselves (Mark 12:31). In the church, we tend to focus so much on loving others that we fail to realize our ability to love others fully is contingent on our ability to love ourselves. You can't have one without the other. Marriage makes us better because it challenges us to acknowledge what might be holding us back from receiving love, but more so, it invites us to accept that kind of love for ourselves— even when it might feel undeserved. Jesus lavishes His love on us, and invites us to freely partake of it. Not because of who we are, but because of who *He* is. And those who freely receive are those who can freely give (Matthew 10:8). Marriage isn't just about becoming happier; it's about becoming better. But ironically, in becoming better, we often find that we've also become happier. Find true self love first!

*Because marriage teaches commitment.* Author and pastor Tim Keller wrote, "Real love, the Bible says, instinctively desires permanence."[5] Deep down we are all made for lifelong love. We have a deep desire to be known, and to be loved, for life. But when we simply follow our feelings into marriage, we can also follow our feelings right out of marriage. Just as quickly as you can fall in love, you can fall out of love.

Feelings come, and feelings go, and those who build the foundation of their marriage on how they feel will eventually find their marriage crumbling. I choose marriage because although I know my feelings are fickle, my faith is not. My emotions may fail me, but my choices are always up to me. I choose to love, to trust, to forgive, and to remain. It's easy to follow our hearts, but it takes real courage to lead our hearts.

*Because marriage invites you to take responsibility.* In marriage, I am forced to come face-to-face with my junk—from my baggage and mistakes from the past, to the decisions I make, to my responses, reactions, attitudes, and behaviors toward my spouse. Oftentimes we make choices but fail to take responsibility for them. Yet marriage is like a mirror because it reflects what's there. In marriage, another human being is facing us at all times, exposing both our strengths and our struggles just by their presence. And at times, that can cause friction. But that very same friction is what files down our rough edges, forcing us to see the blemishes of our lives and take responsibility for what we need to change.

It's easy to dodge responsibility when there's no one to call us out. We want a free pass, and we quickly blame everything on the other person. But marriage forces us to see there are always two people involved, each of us having to take ownership of our own junk. Galatians 6:5 puts it this way: "Each of you must take responsibility for doing the creative best you can with your own life" (MSG). Simply put, it's your responsibility to do your best with what you have. I am a hundred times better than the person I was when I got married because I have been sharpened and refined by the discipline of learning to take responsibility.

*Because marriage reminds you that you need Jesus.* Oftentimes I find the people struggling the most to enjoy the deep blessing of marriage are the people who have never taken the time to fill themselves. Too many people get so caught up trying to *find* the right "one" that they fail to *become* the right "one" in the process. It's easy to go into marriage feeling half full emotionally, spiritually, and physically, hoping this other person will have what it takes to fill us up. But marriage can't fill us up to overflowing. Only Jesus can. If anything, marriage reveals our emptiness. It can certainly add drops of water to our emotional bucket, but it can never fill us the way we need to be filled. Marriage can bring great blessings, but it first requires us to answer some tough questions while standing alone: Who am I? Where did I come from? What has shaped me and which parts of my life need healing? Where am I headed and what is God's calling on my life? In what ways am I allowing my relationship with Jesus to change me and fill me up?

When we begin to deal with our own shortcomings, we go into marriage more healthy and whole. When we begin to grasp our God-given identity, we go into marriage feeling more at peace and secure. When we catch God's calling on our life and establish a vision for our future, we go into marriage with purpose and direction. When we allow God's love to pour into us, we go into marriage already feeling complete. Ephesians 3:17-19 is a beautiful depiction of this fullness:

> I pray that you, being rooted and established in love, may have power, together with all the Lord's holy people, to grasp how wide and long and high and deep is the love of Christ, and to know this love that surpasses knowledge—that you may be filled to the measure of all the fullness of God.

When Christ's love fills you to the measure of all the fullness of God, your fullness begins to overflow into the lives of those around you. There is no greater joy than giving and receiving love out of our overflow rather than trying to give love out of our scarcity. Going into marriage with a full heart gives us the opportunity to experience the ecstasy of *real* love.

*Because marriage is so much bigger than you.* As a Christian, I realize my marriage is not just about me. It's so much bigger than me and so much bigger than my husband. God uses the analogy of marriage to describe His love for His people for a reason: in marriage we get a glimpse of a love that's far bigger than us. Our desire for love reflects a universal need for love, for commitment, and for something and *Someone* greater than ourselves. Through the unique covenant of marital love, we're invited to get a glimpse of the great and unconditional love of God.

Not only that, but my marriage is bigger than me because it affects those around me. So many lives are shaped by this one commitment between two people—most significantly for us, the lives of our three precious children. At this stage, our marriage is the primary definition

*[handwritten margin note: God loves me more than any earthy love I will ever feel.]*

of love they get to see. Not only do we owe it to ourselves to live out love, but we owe it to them. How we reflect the giving and receiving of love will make an impact on generations to come.

## What Will You Choose?

When the rubber meets the road and we're faced with the difficult choices that come with two people becoming one, we're given every excuse and every reason to walk away rather than do the work. We find ourselves wondering, *Is this worth it? Is it worth the pain? Is it worth the work? Is it worth the energy, time, emotions, sacrifice, and commitment?* You might be wrestling with those same questions right now. Maybe you're in a marriage that has become very difficult to navigate. Maybe you're dealing with bruised emotions, broken hearts, and feeling like you've got nothing left to give.

Or maybe you're reading this book as someone from the outside looking in. You're jaded at the idea of marriage because you've seen so many people struggling along the way. People talk about how marriage is hard—how you lose your love after the honeymoon stage, how you'll at some point want to get a divorce, how every day is an effort to connect and stay in love. If marriage is so hard, you wonder, why even bother?

Why choose the hard thing when you could coast through life without it?

## The Hardest and Greatest

A healthy marriage isn't defined by the word *hard*. While there are hard moments, in and of itself, *hard* isn't an accurate description of the journey marriage takes you on. If marriage was just hard, no one would ever do it. Marriage is so much more. It's a journey marked by joy and adventure. It's filled with laughter, and fun, and togetherness, and vulnerability, and humility, and forgiveness, all built upon layers and layers of grace. It's an unrivaled intimacy between two people supernaturally becoming one. Marriage has the potential of being the deepest and most fulfilling relationship you will ever experience on the face of this earth. *Nothing* in this world compares to the joys of a good marriage.

I know a precious couple who live out the reality of the deep joy of a good marriage. Even as a child, I remember watching them interact with nothing less than admiration and fondness toward each other. They would take daily strolls hand in hand and tell stories of sleeping outside underneath the stars, snuggling in each other's embrace. They were inseparable, and their oneness was evident to everyone who interacted with them. Even after raising three children, moving across the country, and dealing with major tragedy, they continued to cling to both God and each other in the most passionate way. And to this day they are still desperately enthralled with each other.

> A good marriage comes from a series of decisions over an extended period of time, with the commitment of two people choosing to love each other no matter what may come their way.

*Thank God for this!*

A good marriage is an enormous blessing. And it doesn't just happen to the lucky ones. A good marriage comes from a series of decisions over an extended period of time, with the commitment of two people choosing to love each other no matter what may come their way.

But even in the happiest marriages come moments of hard. Moments of struggle, and selfishness, and sin. Moments of anger, and hurt, and pain. Moments when we want to throw in the towel. Moments when loving takes will, and liking takes work. Moments made up of simple daily choices or significant ongoing choices, but nonetheless, moments that require us to choose love.

*marriage represent God's love*

> Love is very patient and kind, never jealous or envious, never boastful or proud, never haughty or selfish or rude. Love does not demand its own way. It is not irritable or touchy. It does not hold grudges and will hardly even notice when others do it wrong. It is never glad about injustice, but rejoices whenever truth wins out. If you love someone, you will be loyal to him no matter what the cost. You will always believe in him, always expect the best of him, and always stand your ground in defending him (1 Corinthians 13:4-7 TLB).

Sometimes loving, *truly loving*, is straight-up difficult! But to dig deep, to choose kindness, to seek forgiveness, to call on grace, to admit our wrongs, to confess our weaknesses, to keep no record of wrong, to come together, to choose love, to *receive* love...those are the moments when we get to experience what miracles are made of. Those are the moments when we're asked to give out of what we don't have, by tapping into what God has for us. And what He has is an abundance of grace, an overflow of mercy, and a fountain of forgiveness. And what He has is always enough.

## Choosing Marriage

We live in a culture that despises the idea of sacrifice. We're taught to strive for power, control, and the upper hand in a relationship. We're told to do what "feels right" and not to tolerate anything less. We're fooled into thinking that love is only about what makes us happy. And the moment we feel less than happy, we're encouraged to bail. To abandon ship. To stop investing.

But culture has got it all wrong.

The more we give, the better we become. And the better we become, the better our marriages become.

There is no greater love than one of sacrifice. We see this kind of love so clearly evidenced in Scripture, modeled to us by Jesus, the greatest Lover of all, who laid down His life to open wide the doors to a relationship with Him. And for us to experience real love, we're asked to do the same. "Greater love has no one than this, that someone lay down his life" (John 15:13 ESV). In choosing marriage, we're offered an invitation to experience the greatest kind of earthly love ever known to mankind, the closest example of Christ's deep love for every one of us. — *Do I love Patrick in this way? Like Christ?*

My hope and prayer for this book is that it will encourage and inspire you, no matter what your current relationship status, to choose love, to choose marriage. At the heart of it, experiencing real love requires us to also experience real sacrifice. It requires us to give of ourselves in big ways and small.

It's about offering forgiveness when you've been hurt.

It's about giving your time though it's not always convenient.

It's about sharing your heart when you'd rather hold back.

It's about cleaning the kitchen after a long day even when it's your least favorite job.

It's about choosing to respond with love when you'd rather respond in anger.

It's about offering a listening ear when you'd rather tune out or go to bed.

It's about giving up that last bite of cake so your spouse can enjoy it.

It's about putting someone else's needs and desires before your own.

It's about learning to receive love and forgiveness and grace just as you learn to give it.

The list could go on and on, but the sacrifice always ends with the same formula: *we > me*. It always forces us to choose self or to choose marriage. And the choice to love is yours for the making.

> Love is a temporary madness. It erupts like an earth-quake and then subsides. And when it subsides you have

to make a decision. You have to work out whether your roots have become so entwined together that it is inconceivable that you should ever part. Because this is what love is. Love is not breathlessness, it is not excitement, it is not the promulgation of promises of eternal passion. That is just being "in love" which any of us can convince ourselves we are. Love itself is what is left over when being in love has burned away.[6]

Are you willing to take a step of grace in choosing love? Are you ready to take a step of faith in choosing marriage? Are you willing to allow these daily choices to transform you into the best version of yourself, and in turn, to transform your relationship? If the answer is yes, then I rejoice with you for choosing marriage, the *hardest* and *greatest* thing you'll ever do.

## REFLECTION QUESTIONS FOR MARRIED COUPLES

1. What have been the hardest parts of marriage? What have been the greatest parts of marriage?

2. "Marriage is like a mirror because it reflects what's there." What has marriage reflected, or revealed, to you about yourself?

3. On a scale of 1–10 (10 being the most), how "full" do you feel emotionally? Spiritually? What are some areas in your life that need healing? In what ways can you apply Ephesians 3:17-19 to your life? What are some healthy ways you can take responsibility for "getting filled up"?

# REFLECTION QUESTIONS
## FOR SINGLES

1. What are some of the hard things you've witnessed in marriages around you? What are some of the great things?

2. On a scale of 1–10 (10 being the most), how "full" do you feel emotionally? Spiritually? What are some areas in your life that need healing? In what ways can you apply Ephesians 3:17-19 to your life? What are some healthy ways you can take responsibility for "getting filled up"?

3. What do you look forward to in marriage? What are some of your fears?

# 2

# We > Me

*From Selfishness to Holiness*

Very few people know exactly what they're getting into when it comes to getting married. My sweet grandmother was certainly no exception. Just today I was on the phone with her, listening to her fondly reminisce with laughter in her voice about how "clueless" she was. Growing up in Cairo, Egypt, she and my grandfather entered a semi-arranged marriage when they were just teenagers. Suddenly she found herself the wife of a passionate young evangelist who wanted nothing more than to tell the world about Jesus. They knew nothing of marriage, family, or parenting. They hardly knew each other! There were no marriage books to read, marriage seminars to attend, or pre-marital counseling sessions to enroll in. There was nothing but trial and error, covered in a whole lot of love, commitment, prayer, and a whole lot more of God's grace. They were married for over 60 beautiful years before he went to be with Jesus. But looking back, she'll be the first to admit their loving marriage was certainly not a testament to how much they knew, but rather to the incredible grace of a loving God in the lives of two young people who knew so very little.

Even with the little knowledge we have before marriage, most of us have some sort of an idea of what marriage will be like. We have hopes, dreams, and expectations for how it will look. We watch movies, read books, idolize TV shows, and even observe marriages around us to get a glimpse of this thing we call holy matrimony. But we don't really know until we're there, do we? I understood some things about marriage going into it, but so many things I never could have imagined. And to this day, over a decade into it, there's so much left to learn. For example, some say marriage teaches you more about selflessness than you ever wanted to know. I've come to realize that's true. I mean, I knew I had the ability to be selfish, but I didn't know I was truly selfish until I became a wife.

Let's start with the small things most people don't really think about before getting married. We talk openly and freely about the concept of "two becoming one," but do we ever consider these things: One house? One bed? One bathroom? One mirror above one bathroom sink? One bank account? One budget? One remote control? All those ones leave a whole lot of room for selfishness when divided between two people.

## Bathroom Drama

Speaking of small things, let's talk bathrooms for a moment, shall we? I mean, I personally never could have imagined the plethora of conversations that could stem from a bathroom. Let me give you a front-row seat into our "lavatory personality types" (and no, that's not a clinical term, but it should be).

Walk into our bathroom and, if you know us, you'll instantly identify which side of the sink is mine and which is John's. You won't identify these respective sides because they're labeled or because we have pink towels hanging on my side and blue towels hanging on his. You'll identify them because my side is an organized disaster and his side is as tidy as the day we moved in. And trust me, some invisible boundaries exist on this countertop. Every now and again, when my side starts creeping into his, he'll take a second and make sure to push everything back onto my side. The makeup, the straightening iron, the hair serums, the bobby pins, the toiletries—everything.

But even though I'm a little more creative in my countertop appearance, I still know where everything is and I believe everything should have its place (even if "its place" vaguely means on the left side of the sink right next to the lotion). So when I open the bathroom closet and see his pants hanging right over my full-length mirror, exactly the place where pants do not belong, I make sure to take those pants and put them elsewhere. Which causes him to put them back over the mirror. Which causes me to put them elsewhere yet again. Which causes us both to go batty. And on and on the bathroom drama goes.

And let's not forget the toilet paper. John is the king of leaving the toilet paper roll either completely empty and still in the dispenser, or worse yet, with about, oh, one tiny little square left. Then again, I'm the queen of going halfway and getting a new roll, but then being too lazy to replace the empty roll. So I end up just propping the new roll on the empty one. Frankly, when it comes to bathroom drama, I'm not sure which one of us is more annoying. But ten years into marriage, we've at least finally agreed on the type of toilet paper we both like to use.

Even as I'm writing this, I find myself smiling, thinking about our different quirks and bathroom habits, and I've only just begun to scratch the surface here. But the thing about all of this is selflessness begins in the small things. It begins with a heart that's willing to overlook which way you'd like the toilet paper roll to face, or how often pants are hanging on a door, or the makeup avalanche that's about to overtake your side of the sink. It begins with a heart that's willing to say "we before me" in big things, but mostly in small things. Proverbs 19:11 gives the much-needed reminder that "sensible people control their temper; they earn respect by overlooking wrongs" (NLT).

In marriage, you relearn the preschool lessons of sharing in a very non-preschool kind of way. You spend your entire life as a single person with only one person to think about: yourself. You get to decide what you'll eat, what you'll wear, where you'll go, how you'll spend your money, and exactly what you want to do with your time and energy. But suddenly, you're faced with someone who brings to your life a whole new set of desires, needs, habits, quirks, opinions, and ideas. And only selflessness can bridge the gap, transforming your differences into your greatest assets.

## Selfless Versus Passive

Since I've referenced the word *overlook*, I want to make sure there's no misunderstanding here of what overlooking an offense means. We need to take the time to really delve into the difference between being "passive" and being "selfless," because many people get this wrong in their relationships, which can lead to major devastation.

### Jennifer's Story

Jennifer was a conflict avoider. When she came to my office looking for marriage advice, the first thing that stood out to me was how much she had bottled up inside. She sat down and spilled the beans about everything her husband was doing (and not doing) that was having a negative impact on her, and in turn, on their marriage. He was critical, perfectionistic, and was on her about every little thing. And when he didn't get his way? He would withdraw in irritation and anger until things blew over. Then he was back to acting like nothing happened.

In her efforts to keep the peace, she decided she was just going to stay quiet and let things go. She would listen to his rants and do her best to accommodate, without ever taking the time to express her personal needs or emotions. But as I pointed out to her, a person can absorb only so much conflict until it finally needs a way to escape. And eventually, like lava spilling from a volcano, it will find the path of least resistance. Sure enough, there would come a time when Jennifer could take it no more, and she'd burst into a puddle of tears, feeling helpless and frustrated. But instead of expressing her emotions and dealing with the situation, her cycle of letting things go simply started again.

Jennifer was confusing selflessness with passivity. It's a pattern we could also trace into other parts of her life. In unpacking her relationship history and talking through her past, she concluded she had been a passive person for a majority of her life. Let's be clear: there isn't anything selfless about absorbing conflict, accepting criticism, or allowing someone to treat you with disrespect—not even your spouse. If selflessness is defined as considering the needs of others, it's certainly *not* defined by failing to consider ourselves. We need to get this aspect of selflessness right, because a life of passivity will do as much damage to our relationships as a life of selfishness.

## What Selflessness Is Not

How do you recognize if you're truly selfless or just passive? How do you know if you're putting the needs of others first or simply not considering your own? As with most relationships and interactions, there are no hard-and-fast rules or magical formulas to becoming selfless. But there are signs to look for that can give you insight into your typical pattern of interacting with people. Let's start with what selflessness is *not*:

*Always saying yes:* I use a little "get-to-know-you" activity with my clients. I give them two words—like *teacher* or *student, mountain* or *valley, hammer* or *nail*—and ask them to choose the one that best describes them and explain why. There are no right or wrong answers; this exercise is about reflecting and describing oneself. One of the sets of words on the list is *yes* or *no. Are you a yes person or a no person?* Too many times people confuse selflessness with "always saying yes," when that's simply not the case.

Selflessness doesn't mean we ignore our limits. Selflessness doesn't mean we push ourselves to the point of feeling stretched too far and spread too thin. Selflessness doesn't mean we can't say no. Selflessness doesn't mean we don't have boundaries. Living a life that always says yes to every request that comes our way will leave us feeling drained, frustrated, exhausted, and—ironically—with nothing left to give. Because inevitably, by saying yes to something, we are unwittingly and unknowingly saying no to something else: to our time, to our health, to our energy, or to the quality of our relationships. It's important to be a person of balance, with an ability to discern when to say yes and when to say no.

*Keeping your hurts to yourself:* Have you ever had one of those moments when you're sitting in the car with your spouse and one of you is *obviously* not talking? It usually goes something like this:

"What's the matter?"

"Nothing."

"Are you sure?"

"Yes, I'm fine."

"You're obviously not fine, because you've been sitting quietly for 15 minutes."

"I said I'm *fine*."

And on and on the hopeless conversation goes.

But selflessness does not mean we allow ourselves to slowly die on the altar of saying nothing. It doesn't mean we hide our emotions at the expense of our personal health and well-being. True selflessness is about loving others well, but the vicious truth is that we can't love others well until we've learned to value and respect ourselves.

> You can't hold someone responsible for something you never told them they were responsible for.

*Failing to voice your needs:* I once heard it said that you can't hold someone responsible for something you never told them they were responsible for. I like that concept, because it really identifies the need for healthy communication (much more on this in the next chapter) and our personal responsibility in getting our needs met. We expect people to read our minds, know what we need, and then act on it. And when they fail to do so, we walk away feeling frustrated and hurt. They didn't give us what we never told them we needed! How much sense does that make? Yet all of us struggle with this, and especially within the marriage relationship.

*voice them*

Selflessness does not mean ignoring your needs or keeping them to yourself. It doesn't mean staying silent and expecting others to know what you want or need. And it doesn't mean holding back, particularly when speaking up could be beneficial to your personal health and the health of your relationship. Healthy relationships are defined by give-and-take, and being a person who only gives and never takes is living a passive life, not a selfless one. It's up to you to learn to identify your needs and then express them in a respectful, assertive, and loving way.

## A Cup of Water in the Night

Sometimes it can be just as hard to *receive* selflessness as it is to give it. For some people, the very thought of asking for what they need or allowing others to serve them sacrificially can be a challenge in and of itself. But as I mentioned before, healthy relationships are about give-and-take, so it's just as crucial that we learn to receive love from others in the form of sacrifice, service, and selflessness.

One of my favorite books describes this concept of reciprocity in marriage. In *A Severe Mercy,* author Sheldon Vanauken spends chapter after beautiful chapter poetically portraying the deep romance between him and his wife, Davey. But their passion-filled marriage didn't develop overnight. Rather, it was strengthened one day at a time, one action at a time. Early in the book he describes some of the actions they took to strengthen their relationship, one of which he called "the principle of courtesy." Vanauken described the principle of courtesy as simply this: whatever one person asked the other to do, the other would do. It was that simple. "Thus, one might wake the other in the night, and ask for a cup of water; and the other would peacefully (and sleepily) fetch it...And we considered it a very great courtesy to *ask* for the cup as well as to fetch it."[1]

My family has its own "cup of water" story. My mom's parents were born and raised in Cairo, Egypt. Almost every night, my grandfather would wake up thirsty and ask my grandmother to fetch him a cup of water. Knowing how hard he worked during the day, she would always oblige. Every night she would selflessly leave the comfort of her warm bed and step out into the cold (in the 1960s in Cairo, there was no such thing as in-home heaters). Night after night she found herself engaging in this routine of fetching him a cup of water, until one day she decided she was going to take the more efficient route. Instead of getting out of bed during the cold winter night, she planned ahead and set a pitcher of water and an empty glass next to his bed before they went to sleep.

Late that same night, my grandfather received an unexpected phone call. He fumbled around on his nightstand to grab the rotary phone, only to confuse it with the pitcher of water he didn't realize was there. And he ended up absolutely and completely drenched.

Selflessness is never about convenience;
it's always about sacrifice.

I love this story, not only because it's a funny moment in my grandparents' relationship, but because it offers us a picture of what selflessness looks like in a real marriage—even before the time of home heaters, cell phones, and bottled water. At the end of the day, selflessness is never about convenience; it's always about sacrifice.

## What Selflessness Is

I asked a few friends to share what selflessness looks like in the marriages. Here are some of their answers:

- "Selflessness means his waking up on a Saturday morning to watch the kids so that I can sleep in."
- "Selflessness is when she goes out of her way to make me dinner, when I know she's just as tired as I am."
- "Selflessness is him taking me out for Mexican food, even though he's not a fan, just because he knows it's my favorite."
- "Selflessness is when she agrees to rent an action movie to watch with me on a Friday night, when I know that's her least favorite genre."
- "Selflessness is when he listens and truly values what I have to say, no matter what time of day!"
- "Selflessness is when she takes such great care of me whenever I'm feeling sick, not asking for anything in return."
- "Selflessness is him granting me grace when I have wronged him, and providing gentle correction."
- "Selflessness is when my beautiful bride takes the time to iron my clothes before she leaves for work in the morning, ensuring I'm wrinkle-free for the day."
- "Selflessness is when he chooses to spend his free day walking around the park with me, even though he could be fishing."
- "Selflessness is when I come home after a long day of work to find he's finished all the laundry and dishes, even though I know he had a busy day."

As we see in the broad range of answers above, there isn't a one-size-fits-all description of what selflessness will look like. It takes v relationship. But one theme that comes up

hat selflessness always involves an act of sac-

.c giver, as well as the willingness to accept that

ur the receiver. With that in mind, here are important

_s that will give you some practical ways to choose selfless-

_ss in your relationship.

— *Put your spouse's needs and wants before your own.* Choosing self-lessness in marriage requires that we learn to recognize our spouse's desires and then go out of our way to fulfill those desires to the best of our ability. Philippians 2:4 puts it so well in saying, "Let each of you look not only to his own interests, but also to the interests of others" (ESV). A huge part of understanding our spouse's interests, desires, and needs is by taking initiative to ask them, *What can I do to help? What do you need from me? What would you like to do? Which one would you rather choose?* Taking an active approach to selflessness means we first understand what our spouse's needs, wants, and preferences are and then follow through in fulfilling those things in the ways we can. Even when it's inconvenient, difficult, or out of the way. Even if it's something we would prefer not to do—like fetching a cup of water in the middle of the night.

*Step out of your norm.* A few years ago, when I first launched my relationship blog, I was a complete novice when it came to the ins and outs of running a website. And frankly, so was my husband. With his being in the medical field, and me in the mental health field, it's safe to say we were lacking in our computer science knowledge. But as TrueLoveDates.com evolved from a hobby blog to a wide-reaching ministry, John selflessly stepped up to the plate and decided to learn all things web design and programming. He poured hours into reading books, watching YouTube videos, and scouring message boards to learn everything he needed to know to build and run the behind-the-scenes at TrueLoveDates.com, even though these things were totally outside his normal interests.

Over the past few years, working on this ministry together has truly enriched our relationship, because it connects us in a special way. I think the same principle applies to every marriage when a couple learns to step out of their norm and into the interests and life of their loved one. Maybe it's learning about golf, taking an interest in gardening, or even choosing to travel with our spouse when we'd rather stick to our typical routine. Maybe it's reading a new book, trying a new food, or doing something we wouldn't normally do. But it's in the act of stepping out of our comfort zone that we find our selflessness increased and our relationship enriched.

Our time is limited to 24 hours a day. Subtract from that the hours we sleep, work, and take care of our children, and our free time can often be so little (some days nonexistent). I know far too many couples who decide *not* to step out of their comfort zones and instead choose to consistently engage in separate hobbies, interests, and activities. I'm not saying we can't have our own hobbies and interests every now and again—that's a normal and healthy part of life. But since our free time has the power to bring us closer together as we share things or pull us apart as we stick to what we've always done, it's important for each of us to recognize the areas of our life together that need sacrifice and selflessness. It's important to step out of our comfort zone for the sake of our spouse.

*Learn to compromise.* Speaking of taking steps, let's talk about compromise. Compromise is the act of taking figurative steps toward the other person, deciding to meet in the middle when it's possible to do so. Most of marriage is not made up of "my way or your way" decisions, but rather about finding "our way." It's about each person giving up a little to reach the greater gain of a happy medium.

John and I have significantly different energy levels at various times of the day. He's a morning person and will usually wake up peppy and talkative, ready to conquer the world. The morning finds me as perky as a grumpy bear who was suddenly aroused from hibernation. But nighttime? That's my time to shine. I have my deepest thoughts, most creative moments, and best conversations after nine o'clock at night. But with his crazy medical school schedule early on in our marriage, nine o'clock was pretty much the time his head needed to be hitting the pillow. I remember many nights in our first few years of marriage filled with tears (on my part) and frustration (on his part) because I needed to talk and he needed to sleep. When it came to finding the right bedtime, it was beyond clear that we had to make a compromise.

Going to bed together every night has always been important to both of us, because it's our time to connect, to debrief, and to spend some time together before the day is done. So he gave a little, and I gave a little, and we found a bedtime that allowed us both to feel loved and connected, but also well rested (and as a side note, I learned to invest in a much-needed reading light so my night-owl self could read in bed while he snoozed off peacefully by my side). Sometimes self-lessness is much more practical than we imagine it will be.

## Not Today, Satan

We've discussed what selflessness isn't, and we've discussed what selflessness is. And let me tell you, knowledge of these concepts is the first step, because in life and in marriage, the more you know, the better you do. But in my line of work, I'm aware that some of you might be reading through this chapter and thinking, *Well, that's all well and good when you have a good marriage. It's easy to be selfless when you have a partner who is being selfless back to you.*

I want to take a moment to address those of you who are feeling empty, exhausted, and tired in your marriage. Let me just assure you that every person reading this book (and the one writing it as well) has been there too. Whether for a few moments, hours, days, or even years, it's not uncommon to get to a place in marriage where you feel like you've got nothing left to give, much less engage in selflessness.

I remember one couple who came to me for marriage counseling. After less than five years of marriage, boundaries had been crossed, trust had been broken, and feelings had been hurt. Both husband and wife were feeling emotionally exhausted and spiritually empty. They wanted to get to a better place in their marriage—they just didn't know where to start. They didn't even know if they had it in them. After just a few sessions together, I decided to meet with each of them alone, as I commonly do in marriage counseling. I think sometimes the best thing we can do is take the time to look inward and get ourselves to a better place spiritually and emotionally before we start working on our marriage.

As I talked to each of them, I noticed a theme: they were both completely drained and running on empty. With the demands of work, life, and raising small children, they had not only neglected each other, but they had also neglected themselves in the process. Their emotional health was suffering, their physical health was suffering, and most concerning, their spiritual health was suffering. And when two empty people try to engage in marriage, they end up feeling frustrated, disappointed, and hurt when the other person can't give them what they need.

But truth be told, that is exactly what the Enemy wants us to feel and experience in the context of marriage. He wants to zap us of our hope and fill us with despair. He wants to drain us of our energy, our selflessness, and our ability to love each other the way God calls us to love. The devil is a liar and a deceiver and the enemy of all that is good in this world (1 Peter 5:8). He is waiting to pounce on our marriages because he knows that when they are done well, they are a glorious reflection of God's deep love to the world (Ephesians 5:31-32). Whether or not you are aware of it, a major spiritual battle is going on right now, smack-dab in the middle of your home. "Our struggle is not against flesh and blood," says Paul, "but against the rulers, against the authorities, against the powers of this dark world and against the spiritual forces of evil in the heavenly realms" (Ephesians 6:12).

So much more is at stake than we realize. Brothers and sisters, a full-fledged spiritual battle is taking place in our marriages. And these spiritual battles have less to do with where we've come from and more to do with where we could be. The Enemy is on high alert because he sees the potential our marriages have to become great. He knows the great blessing a marriage can be. He understands the powerful message of God's love that a good marriage will reflect to a lost and dying world, and he'll do anything and everything he can to keep that from happening. We must continue to fight this battle and walk toward victory in Christ. It's up to each of us to look Satan in the eye and proclaim, "Not today, Satan," with every selfless action we take and every selfless decision we choose. Satan is the enemy, *not* our spouse. God wants to strengthen us for the unseen spiritual and emotional battles we will face in marriage, but the only way we can prepare is by exchanging our emptiness for God's fullness.

## The One and Only

When I was a young girl, my dad told me a story about a well. He said, "Human beings are like wells. Every time we interact with someone, we take a little bit of our water to give them something to drink. But over time, if we continue to give from our well without ever filling it up, we eventually hit the bottom of our well, and run out of fresh water—we find that we've got nothing left to give but mud."

In my field of work, it's easy to give, and give, and give without personally recognizing my need to get filled up again. But filling my well isn't something my husband can do for me. It's not something my children can do for me. It's not something my family or friends can do for me. Oh, they can certainly add sweet drops of water into my life, but as far as filling up my well, only one relationship can do that for me—or for any of us.

Simply put, our relationship with Jesus is the one and only relationship that can fill up our wells to the point of overflowing. In understanding and receiving His deep love for us, we allow ourselves to be filled up in a way that only God can do, because it's not of ourselves—it's supernatural. And out of that overflow of love we have what we need to give, to serve, to sacrifice, and to move from selfishness to holiness.

Within the context of our relationship with Christ, we get a front-row seat to sacrificial love displayed toward us, in the form of Jesus laying down His very life in exchange for one thing: relationship with us. Oh, what deep, deep love! When we can finally grasp that love for us, we gain the power and motivation we need to offer that same self-less love to another. Imagine what that could do in our lives. Imagine what that could do in our relationships. Imagine what that could do in our marriages.

My prayer for you reading this book today is that no matter how empty your well may feel, your understanding of God's love for you will move from logical to experiential. No matter how thirsty you are in your life and in your marriage right now, I pray that you will come to the waters of Christ and *receive*. In the book of Isaiah, the Lord gives a beautiful invitation to those who are thirsty:

> Come, all you who are thirsty, come to the waters; and you who have no money, come, buy and eat! Come, buy wine and milk without money and without cost. Why spend money on what is not bread, and your labor on what does not satisfy? Listen, listen to me, and eat what is good, and you will delight in the richest of fare (Isaiah 55:1-2).

*Come*, says our Lord. Come and be satisfied. You don't have to earn it. You don't have to buy it. You don't even have to deserve it. You simply have to receive it. Because only through the love of our God can you be *filled*.

Filled enough to give.

Filled enough to serve.

Filled enough to sacrifice.

Filled enough to move from selfishness to holiness.

Filled enough to choose marriage. Because *choosing marriage has the power to make you better along the way.*

## REFLECTION QUESTIONS
## FOR MARRIED COUPLES

1. Which of these practical acts of selflessness do you need to practice in your marriage?

    a. Putting my spouse's needs and wants before my own.

    b. Stepping out of my norm/comfort zone.

    c. Learning to compromise.

2. What are two specific ways you can display selflessness toward your spouse this week?

3. Review "What Selflessness Is Not." Do you tend to mistake passivity for selflessness? If so, which area do you struggle with the most? What are some steps you can take to express your emotions and needs to your spouse?

4. How are you investing in your relationship with God and allowing Him to fill you up?

## REFLECTION QUESTIONS
## FOR SINGLES

1. In your family, friendships, and closest relationships, do you tend to mistake passivity for selflessness? If so, what are some steps you can take to express your emotions and needs in a healthy way?

2. In preparing yourself for healthy relationships and

learning to identify passivity, which of these areas do you need to work on?

   a. Always saying yes.

   b. Keeping your hurts to yourself.

   c. Failing to voice your needs.

3. How are you investing in your relationship with God and allowing Him to fill you up?

3

# Walls Will Fall

*From Vulnerability to Intimacy*

We all come to relationships with walls—barriers we possess in need of being broken or taken down. Things we've used to protect ourselves, to defend ourselves, and to keep us from getting hurt. Ways we keep people at a distance, or even keep them out. We all have walls. We just don't always recognize them.

Some walls are obvious. I homeschool my children, and the other week we somehow got onto the topic of the Great Wall of China. One thing you might not know about the Great Wall is that it's not just one big wall—it's a series of many walls, sometimes running parallel to one another.[1] Mile after mile of brick, stone, and wood, the Great Wall of China is one of the most extensive barriers ever constructed in our world, with much of it still standing today. Originally, it was built to protect China from enemies and intruders.

But the most interesting thing about this Great Wall of China is that, ultimately, it never really served its intended purpose. It didn't prevent invaders from entering China. But it *did* come to function "as a psychological barrier between Chinese civilization and the world, and remains a powerful symbol of the country's enduring strength."[2] As I said before, some walls are obvious.

But other walls are much subtler. I once heard about the process of training elephants in the circus. To keep an elephant from escaping or even trying to get away, the trainers would tie a rope around one of its legs shortly after birth and tie the other end of the rope to a stake in the ground. The baby elephant would then be allowed to roam freely, though it couldn't go beyond the radius of the rope. When it reached the end of the rope's radius, the baby elephant would feel a tug on its leg from the tension of the rope tied to the stake and quickly learn it could go only that far. After a few months, the baby elephant would grow bigger and stronger, until it was much stronger than the little rope tied around its leg. But it had grown so accustomed to its barrier that it never even tried to pass it, even though it could. Some walls are subtle.

In our lives as well, some walls are big, strong, and fierce like the Great Wall of China, telling everyone around us to keep away. They might come in the form of anger, rage, or yelling. But other times we live with walls that are so subtle we barely even notice them, and like the baby elephant, we continue living with constraints and barriers we hardly know exist. Those walls might quietly make their way into our lives in the form of withdrawing, isolating, or even shutting down. Either way—obvious or subtle—they are there, making their appearance predominantly in the way we act and interact with the people closest to us, keeping us from experiencing the depth and richness of relationships the way God meant for us to experience them.

## From Past to Present

So many factors influence the walls we build and the way we interact with the people around us. One of those influencing factors is our family of origin. So much of what we learn about love stems from how love was given and received in the context of our family. We learn to love based on how love was modeled to us. Just watching our parents interact can have a profound impact on how we learn to interact in our relationships.

Modern psychology has identified elements from a person's childhood that directly influence their interpersonal skills in their present relationships, such as how their parents communicated, how their parents resolved marital problems, and how much responsibility each parent took in resolving conflict. We are creatures of habit, and so much of what we learn is based on what was modeled to us. Whether or not we're actively aware of it, our interpersonal skills are shaped just by observing how those closest to us interact.

But at times in our lives we experience, observe, and then adopt unhealthy interactions. *This must be how it's done*, we find ourselves unconsciously believing. We spin around and around in circles of negative behaviors and interactions that have been passed down to us. And just like that baby elephant, we go into autopilot, doing the same things every day without ever questioning if we can break free from those patterns of interaction, no matter how harmful or destructive they might be. *This is just who I am*, we think, not realizing that our chance to break free of these negative patterns is literally only one step away. In marriage, we can begin the process of breaking down our walls, but to do so, we must first recognize that they exist.

## What Walls?

Many individuals go years, or even the entirety of their lives, without ever recognizing that they have walls in need of fixing, barriers that have been slowly erected around their hearts one brick at a time. You might be reading this and wondering, *What are my walls? Do I even have them?* The answer is yes. We all have them. It's just a matter of learning to identify them. Because unrecognized, these walls make a huge impact on the quality of our relationships.

Sigmund Freud identified patterns of behavior people exhibit to defend themselves. He referred to them as "defense mechanisms." In his observations, Freud identified 17 different defense mechanisms, patterns of behavior that emerged in how people acted and reacted within the context of life and relationships.[3] He broke down these defense mechanisms into distinct categories, but for the sake of simplicity we'll categorize them as "healthy" and "unhealthy" defense mechanisms.

Many actions bring us closer to the people around us. Some of the healthy defense mechanisms commonly referred to in counseling and psychology are forgiveness, altruism, acceptance, mercy, moderation, patience, emotional-regulation, gratitude, respect, and humility. Sound like familiar traits? That's because they are found all throughout the Bible! One portion of Scripture that identifies these important traits is a familiar passage from Galatians: "The fruit that the Spirit produces in a person's life is love, joy, peace, patience, kindness, goodness, faithfulness, gentleness, and self-control" (5:22-23 ERV). The beautiful thing affirmed through this list is that so much of psychology points back to the truths found in Scripture. Psychology and faith go hand in hand because no one understands how human beings function better than the God who fashioned and designed us!

Unhealthy defense mechanisms are ways of interacting and behaving that are damaging to our relationships, such as isolation, denial, withdrawal, invalidation, displacement, fantasy, and passive aggression. These traits are often so ingrained in us that we have no idea we're doing them until someone points it out (namely, and most often, our spouse). These are the walls I refer to by taking some of the insight from Freud's work and putting my own twist on them based on what I've learned and observed in working with hundreds of couples over time. We have unknowingly built so many walls to protect ourselves, but in doing so, we end up harming our relationships and keeping our loved ones out.

### Randall and Veronica

Randall and Veronica had been married for nearly 20 years and had two young adult children. Coming from strong religious roots, for them to divorce was not an option. Instead they chose to "divorce" their hearts from each other within the context of their marriage. Year after year they continued to ignore the walls that were slowly rising between them. But eventually they could ignore them no more. They had reached a point when their walls were so high that they barely interacted outside of fighting and arguing. They had kept each other out for so long that they felt they didn't even know each other anymore. They were both experiencing stress and pain. They needed each other more than ever before, but they continued to choose isolation rather than reaching out. They were both hiding behind their walls.

## The Wall of Isolation

Isolation is a common wall we tend to build around ourselves. Like Randall and Veronica, rather than choosing to be vulnerable with our feelings and with each other, we put our emotions in a box and keep them to ourselves. We know how we feel; we just choose not to share those feelings. This wall is found most in those moments when something seems wrong but no one is willing to talk about it. Maybe we choose to hold back feelings, or maybe we've never learned how to express them. But either way, feelings are the deepest part of a person, and the less we share them with each other, the more isolated we begin to feel.

The problem is we tend to isolate ourselves from our spouse and, instead, we run to others to fill those important emotional needs. We often turn to our family, friends, or even acquaintances, and they become the people we open up to rather than the person who is most important in our lives. But one thing I've observed is that human beings have only so much emotional reservoir built up. Once we share our emotions with someone outside our marriage, we have less of a need to share them within our marriage. So the more we vent to others, the less we find ourselves desiring or needing to share our hearts with our spouse. Beware of innocently building a wall of isolation between you and your spouse.

## The Wall of Denial

> In every conflict that involves two people, both people must ultimately take responsibility for their portion for there to be healthy resolution.

If isolation is failing to share our emotions with our spouse, then denial is when we fail to take responsibility within the context of our conflict. Have you ever been in an argument and convinced yourself that this situation has absolutely nothing to do with you? Or that you have done nothing wrong? If you can answer yes to that question, then you carry the wall of denial. Every single problem, conflict, or argument we face in our marriages has *something* to do with us. We might play a huge role in some situations, and in others we might play a smaller role, but in every conflict that involves two people, both people must ultimately take responsibility for their portion for there to be healthy resolution.

I take this wall very seriously in my counseling practice because if a person can't take some sort of responsibility in their marriage, then there is a bigger problem of pride that needs to be broken down (more on this in the next chapter). Whether I'm dealing with a case like Randall and Veronica's, where there's more of a 50/50 split in responsibility, or a harder case involving infidelity or addictions where the responsibility split is less even, there is absolutely no situation in which the responsibility split is 0/100. Never. Ever. Ever.

This might be hard for some of you to hear, especially those of you who have been on the receiving end of major hurt and pain in marriage. But for us to enter into true healing, we must first become aware of our true responsibility, even if that responsibility simply means acknowledging that we gave too much, enabled a problem to continue, or didn't set proper boundaries. Every dance, no matter how good, bad or ugly, always has two dancers. Don't allow yourself to be fooled by the wall of denial, because it will prevent you from moving toward healing.

## The Wall of Withdrawal

The wall of withdrawal is the tendency to run away instead of deal with the issues that need to be dealt with. It's that "fight or flee" mentality when we're faced with a difficult situation and have to make a decision on how we'll handle it. And typically, there are two kinds of people in this world: those who fight and those who flee. When presented with the two options, the average person might assume it's better to be a person who "flees" than a person who "fights." I mean, no one wants to be a fighter, right? It's better to avoid conflict and confrontation.

Absolutely *wrong*. Fighting is an important part of a healthy relationship, because fighting is a natural consequence of two different people becoming one. And fighting can be done well. What is more concerning in a marriage relationship is a person who is constantly fleeing uncomfortable emotions or evading difficult conversations.

I worked with a couple who had a tough time expressing their true feelings to each other. They were facing stress upon stress in their marriage, but rather than dealing with those stresses by engaging in conversation, they would withdraw from communication. He distracted himself from feeling negative emotions by satiating himself with his addiction to pornography, and she with her addiction to food. But after close to a decade of distraction and withdrawal, their marriage began crumbling to pieces.

When I met them, they were on the brink of divorce without having had one real argument. People who never argue or disagree are typically people who are withdrawing and avoiding conflict rather than dealing with it head-on. But you can hold back the hard conversations for only so long before the dam of bitterness breaks and the floods of contempt destroy your marriage.

Whenever I meet with a couple for premarriage counseling, I always ask about how they handle conflict. The couples who can identify how and then talk me through their conflict are ahead of the game. It's the ones who say they never have conflict that concern me the most. That just means someone is withdrawing. Someone is holding back their feelings, opinions, and ideas rather than choosing to express themselves. And continually withdrawing from a relationship is far more dangerous than any conflict could ever be, because it can signify fear, an inability to deal with difficult emotions, or even apathy. Don't let the wall of withdrawal keep you away from the most meaningful relationships in your life.

## The Wall of Displacement

I always remember the wall of displacement because of a vivid example I heard in one of my undergraduate psychology classes. Displacement is when we take out our negative emotions on someone who doesn't deserve them. The specific example they gave was a man who has a rough day at work and then comes home and kicks the dog. Poor little undeserving puppy! Something about that analogy just makes us feel sad (especially for you animal lovers out there). But what's even more concerning is that we often do this same thing to the people closest to us and don't feel bad about it. Maybe we don't kick our spouse physically, but we often kick them emotionally by placing on them the negative emotions we're carrying. Emotions they did nothing to deserve.

I'm convicted here, because I did this less than 24 hours ago. Let me give you an example of what *not* to do. Yesterday I was home with three sick kids. Anyone who has been home with one sick kid knows taking that level of misery and stress and multiplying it by three equals an overwhelming amount of emotional strain and utter exhaustion. All three kids needed me at all times of the day, and sometimes all at once. Runny noses, throwing up, and diaper changes in between feeding, dressing, and entertaining—all multiplied by three—was a full day, to say the least. Then my husband called me on his way home from work (30 minutes late, mind you). By that point I was so emotionally drained and physically exhausted that I immediately found something to be annoyed about the second he didn't say exactly what I needed him to say.

By the time he walked in the door, I was irritable, withdrawn, and downright cold toward him. In the moment, it felt justified to be perturbed, but looking back I realize that my emotional reaction was not at all equivalent to the situation. My husband may not have responded exactly as I wanted him to, but mostly, he was just at the wrong place at the wrong time. I was taking my stress, exhaustion, and emptiness and displacing it on him. Thankfully, ten years into marriage, we know enough about ourselves, each other, and how we each react to life that we were able to recognize the displacement, talk about it, and move on quickly after I apologized, which is much better than we would have done in our first year of marriage. The more you understand about your walls, the faster you'll be able to recognize them and then let them down in exchange for intimacy.

### The Wall of Invalidation

Some walls can be obvious—like when I displaced my negative feelings onto my husband. But some walls are a little trickier to recognize because they come in the form of not saying something when we should. While this wall is not considered a defense mechanism, it's a dangerous habit I often see in the couples I counsel. The wall of invalidation is when we fail to recognize, acknowledge, speak out, or communicate the good things in the people around us. It's amazing how we can get so good at pointing out flaws in others, but so terrible at pointing out their strengths. It's easy to focus on the negative things around us, or the things that need to be changed, all the while completely ignoring all that is good. It can happen when we say something negative instead of something positive. For example, you spend hours cleaning the house and your spouse walks in only to say nothing about the cleanliness but comments right away about the kids' toys all over the floor.

Invalidation occurs when we repress the positive things and instead convey the negative things. But it can also happen when we choose to say nothing at all. Take that same scenario, but this time your spouse walks in and says absolutely nothing. Rather than saying, "Wow, the house looks amazing! This must have taken hours to clean. Thanks so much—I really appreciate your hard work," your spouse says nothing or changes the subject completely. In either instance, invalidation is damaging because it's repressing the good in exchange for something less desirable: criticism, or often just as damaging, saying nothing at all. Beware of building the wall of invalidation.

## The Wall of Fantasy

Fantasy is another subtle wall we tend to build around ourselves, quietly running to it when life gets too hectic to handle. Fantasy is not necessarily sexual in nature, although it can be. Fantasy simply means anything we use to escape from the reality of life. It can be sexual in nature and blatantly harmful, like pornography or sleazy romance novels. But it can also be something more benign and "acceptable," like working too much, spending too much, or eating too much. It can come in the form of something meaningful, like a hobby, ministry, or career, or something less meaningful, like social media, video games, or binge-watching Netflix. But one thing is clear about the wall of fantasy: it allows for something less important to take the place of what's most important—your marriage. It's an outlet for escaping from reality when you should be engaging in reality. It's found in those moments when you know you should be talking, communicating, and interacting, but instead you choose to escape.

I think this wall has become harder to recognize because it's so enmeshed with how our society functions. Observe any social gathering, and you'll find at least half the people escaping from reality by looking at their phones rather than having real conversation. We've become so good at exchanging the intimate for the inanimate, the real-life connections for something (or someone) that's fake. Beware of the wall of fantasy, because it often creeps in and takes over in such a subtle and unrecognizable way.

### The Wall of Passive-Aggression

The next wall is the one that leads to many of the communication problems people face in marriages today. It's the wall of passive-aggression: the *inability or unwillingness* to say what you mean in a respectful way. Oftentimes people are wired to be either passive (not saying anything) or aggressive (disrespectfully saying what they need) in their communication styles. But passive-aggression comes when instead of using positive, direct words to communicate our needs, we default to indirect, unhealthy, and negative behaviors. Here are some real-life examples of what that looks like played out in a marriage:

- Instead of directly telling your spouse you'd rather not go on that vacation, you keep your feelings in and instead act rude, withdrawn, and distant the entire week.

- Rather than acknowledge that you don't have the time or energy to do something, you agree to do it and then procrastinate getting it done or fail to do it at all.

- After a conflict, you say you are not upset but then go around the house slamming doors, throwing things, or acting irritable and withdrawn.

In each of the situations above the pattern is the same: words that don't match up with actions. The wall of passive-aggression is dangerous in marriage because it makes it impossible for healthy communication to occur for the simple reason that what you say and what you do are two completely different things. For there to be any hope of being understood in a relationship, we must learn to align our actions with our words—to say what we mean, and mean what we say.

### The Wall of Rage

The last wall I want to bring up is the wall of rage. Though it's not categorized as a defense mechanism, it's a common wall people tend to build. It's built brick by brick through a series of emotions that go unnoticed or unidentified. Anger is the negative feeling that accompanies this wall. In and of itself, anger is not bad—it's simply a sign that something is going on that needs to be dealt with or expressed. We call anger a "secondary emotion," meaning deep down, underneath anger, there's always another feeling that hasn't been identified or expressed—hurt, embarrassment, frustration, or fear. Underneath anger is something painful that's too hard or too complicated to express, and so we wind up feeling angry.

The Bible reminds us that even in our anger, we're still responsible for making good choices and expressing our anger in a way that avoids sin (Ephesians 4:26). If anger is the root emotion that accompanies this wall, rage is the negative actions and choices of that anger: the yelling, cursing, screaming, and flying off the handle. Rage is that great big, bad lion inside of us that comes out to roar when we've lost all self-control. It often appears when we're too worked up to sit down and understand the other emotions inside of us: namely, the hurt little lamb. Whether or not we realize it, we rage to protect ourselves from getting hurt even more because rage keeps people out.

### Mark and Jenny

When I met Mark and Jenny, they were having some major relationship issues they couldn't seem to get past. They were stuck in a rut of poor communication. In their words, simply put, Jenny was a nag and Mark had rage. She would nag about things, and then he would get angry at the drop of a hat, yelling, screaming, and cursing in ways that caused Jenny to withdraw and shut down. And that's usually the point where their conversation ended. Nothing was getting resolved, only pushed under the rug. But too many things under the rug will eventually cause you to trip. Bit by bit they were feeling more and more separate and alone.

As I always do in my marriage counseling sessions, I asked them to come prepared to talk me through a recent fight they had. I like to get the play-by-play so I can help couples identify their walls and navigate through the hard conversations. That week they came into my office to tell me about their "gardening day." It had been a nice weekend, so they decided to spend the day gardening and pulling weeds. They were working side by side when Jenny noticed a few weeds in the corner that Mark hadn't pulled up yet.

"Make sure to get those weeds, Mark," she said.

No response.

"Are you going to get those?" she asked him.

And just like that, Mark flew off the handle. Within seconds, he was yelling, screaming, and raging at Jenny. "Of course I'm going to get those weeds! Haven't you seen me working hard all day? Do you think I'm incompetent? They're right in my face, and of course I'm going to get them! Do you have to be such a nag about everything?" And just like that their pattern started right back up, both using their walls to hide behind and protect themselves.

I thought this would be a good opportunity to dig a little deeper, so I changed the subject and told Mark to tell me about what feelings it stirs up when Jenny asks him questions like that.

"It makes me feel like she thinks I'm an incompetent fool!"

"Well, that's not a *feeling*, Mark. It's a description of what you think. Which is a good start, but can you try to identify the feeling?" I pressed.

"It makes me feel inadequate. Like I'm not good enough."

With that feeling out in the open, I decided to dig even deeper. Remember, walls are built over *time*—as the patterns we've seen modeled to us or ways we've learned to deal with life are carried over from childhood into adulthood.

Let me give you an example of what that looks like with Mark's story. Later in the session, when things had cooled down a bit, I asked Mark to tell me a little more about that feeling of inadequacy. I asked him if he had ever felt like that in childhood. Mark let out a little chuckle, as though he were remembering something, shook his head a bit, and looked down at the floor. He started telling me about his relationship with his father.

"With my dad, it was 'my way or the highway.' I lived my entire teenage life under his thumb. Nothing I could do was good enough in his eyes, no matter how hard I tried. I was a good kid, and didn't get into much trouble, but it seemed like that wasn't good enough for him. He had an opinion about how I should live every aspect of my life, from my friends, to my education, to my after-school job, to my future career. And if my ideas didn't line up with his ideas, it was over. I never felt good enough for him, and at age 16 I couldn't take that feeling anymore, so I moved out. I've never had a relationship with my dad since that day. I was never good enough for him."

And with that insightful observation, I watched as Mark, this big, strong, bald man covered in tattoos, began to weep like a child right there in the middle of my office, with Jenny watching in complete shock. It was a sobering but powerful moment. And you can believe that this counselor right here shed a few tears with him in that moment too. We were finally beginning to draw the lines connecting the walls that Mark had built from his past all the way to his present. The feelings he had felt of inadequacy were still buried deep inside of him, triggered every time Jenny "nagged him" about something. Her repeated requests made him feel that terrible feeling all over again. But because he was unable to make the connection, he couldn't identify or express how he was really feeling deep down. Instead he would react to that uncomfortable feeling in the only way he knew how: rage.

After we made these connections, Jenny and Mark had a transformation in their relationship. Rather than raging, he would stop and think through how he felt. Rather than withdrawing and isolating, Jenny began to feel empathy for Mark, and her heart softened toward him. She went out of her way to make requests in a way that affirmed him rather than in a way that would demean him. They changed their perception of each other, and their interactions began to change as well. The wall of rage was slowly beginning to come down.

The same choice must be made for you as well. No matter what your specific walls, day by day, they can continue to stand erect in your marriage, or you can choose to bring them down in exchange for open, honest, and vulnerable communication.

## Divorced but Not Divorced

It's truly sad how many Christian couples convince themselves that living a life emotionally "divorced" and disconnected from each other is somehow taking the higher road in marriage. Just because you aren't legally divorced doesn't mean you're living out God's best for your relationship. He wants to help you achieve so much more than the bare minimum. He wants to help you recognize the walls you bring into marriage and the walls that have been built up over time, in order to destroy those walls and begin the process of constructing something far better. He wants to take down our walls of isolation and turn them into bridges of intimacy.

But to do that, we need to willfully accept one important ingredient in our relationship. That is the ingredient of vulnerability—exposing ourselves as we really are, and allowing our spouse the permission to do the same. Vulnerability is the only thing that can begin to tear down the walls we've erected around our hearts and teach us what it means to experience true intimacy.

### Into-Me-See

It is sometimes said that the word *intimacy* should be pronounced "into-me-see," because it requires a level of vulnerability that allows the person before you to peer into your very heart and soul. Something about that thought is extremely romantic, but also terrifying. It's intimidating to imagine a relationship where you can be authentically yourself, loved as you are, because that also means you have to let someone into your deepest places.

But for true intimacy to exist, there must be true vulnerability. There must be a letting down of our walls. There must be the process of building a bridge that invites the person before us to enter our world in a deep and meaningful way. Just like Mark and Jenny in the most recent example, we must be willing to understand and express what's really going on inside of us. And the only thing that has the power to truly bridge that gap is communication. Communication is the lifeline of a relationship. It is the breath of life between two people. Once we stop communicating, our relationship will always begin to die a slow and painful death. That's why walls are so dangerous. They keep us from communicating in an effective and meaningful way.

### The Slow Drifting

If communication is the lifeline of a relationship, when that communication begins to fade, so does the entire relationship. That was exactly what happened for Mike and Susan after nearly two decades of marriage. When I met them in my office, the first sentence that came out of Susan's mouth was, "I feel like we don't even know each other anymore." And she was probably right. Over time, and with the many distractions of life, their communication had begun to slowly fade. Their conversations consisted of superficial things like managing schedules and tag-teaming their children's needs. But the real, intimate conversations had been fading away.

This is often what happens to married couples who aren't intentional about keeping conversation alive. In my survey of over 1000 married people, over 70 percent of couples reported having less than 60 minutes of positive, meaningful conversation per week, with most of those respondents reporting closer to 0-30 minutes of conversation per week. Let me reiterate, we're not talking per day here, but per *week*. This is something people certainly don't expect before getting married. In a comparative survey I took of over 1000 singles, 65 percent of them assumed married couples spend numerous hours per week in positive, meaningful conversation. "Minutes" wasn't even on their radar. Unfortunately, that's far from the truth. To stay connected, two people must be deliberate about moving toward each other, or they'll find themselves slowly drifting.

Every summer we take a family trip to the beach. With three children, we always make it a point to find a quiet spot close to the shoreline so our kids can easily go back and forth between the water and the sand. One day my husband took our two older children to swim and jump waves while I sat under the umbrella with the baby. As I was watching them, I noticed that little by little they started drifting to the left. They didn't notice, because they had their backs to me, but the force of the water and the waves was slowly taking them down the beach. Inch by inch, foot by foot, until eventually they had drifted a block or two away without even realizing it. Eventually, when they were ready to come back to the umbrella to dry off and get a snack, they turned around only to realize I wasn't behind them anymore. Mommy and baby Ezra had been replaced by two sunbathing senior citizens. After looking around for a while, they finally saw me waving and began the long trek back to our spot. That wasn't the first time this had happened, because that's the nature of the ocean. Slowly, the force begins to pull you away without you even realizing it's happening. If you're not deliberate about staying in place, you'll find yourself drifting away.

Marriage is no different. And the thing that keeps you connected more than anything else is your deliberate communication. It's not going to "just happen" unless you take the time to make it happen, even—or should I say, *especially*—when you'd rather do something else.

## The Four Levels of Conversation

Every conversation has a different level of depth, intimacy, and connection based on the content of what's being discussed. The deeper you go conversationally, the more intimate your relationship gets. In my book *True Love Dates*, I discuss these levels in a protective sense, encouraging singles to protect their emotional world by monitoring their levels of conversation and not going too deep, too soon with someone who isn't romantically committed to them. But ironically, often the opposite issue occurs once two people are married. Over time conversation tends to become more and more superficial, and less and less intimate.

*Level 1: Facts.* The first level of conversation is the most basic because it's the kind of conversation you can have with a stranger. It goes into the basic facts of life, answering the questions of who, what, where, when, and why. Facts conversations are a typical part of any marriage because you're constantly connecting about what you're doing, where you're going, or who you're with. *What did you do today? What's the weather this week? Where are you going this afternoon? Where did I put that wallet? Who is going to pick up milk after work? What does your schedule look like? What are your plans?* Whether you're talking about what you watched, read, ate, or saw, facts communication comes with little risk or discomfort because "it is what it is."

*Level 2: Opinions.* The next conversational level is a little deeper, because it offers a little more of yourself. Instead of answering with the basic facts, it goes into the deeper questions of what you think and believe about those facts. It's connected to you because you're revealing your ideas and opinions about the things you're experiencing.

*Which one did you like more? What did you think of dinner? Where would you rather go on vacation? How do you think the meeting went? What did you think about the game last night? Which is your favorite restaurant?* It requires you to give a little more of yourself in offering your thoughts and opinions about the world around you, rather than just reporting the facts.

*Level 3: Feelings.* This level of conversation is where many people get stuck. The ability to talk about your feelings is something the average person has to learn. Contrary to what most people believe, when someone asks, "How was your day?" and you answer by saying, "Good," you aren't sharing your feelings. *Good, fine, okay,* and *bad* aren't feeling words. They are descriptive words (right now I'm imagining someone reading this and looking over to elbow their spouse in that "I told you so" kind of way). I can't tell you how many times I review this when working with clients of all ages. Feeling words express your emotions.

You might have a category of "good" feelings (happy, encouraged, excited, grateful, hopeful, joyful, confident) and a category of "bad" feelings (anxious, hurt, sad, depressed, overwhelmed, frustrated, inadequate), but simply responding "good" or "bad" doesn't tell us how you feel. And most counselors would even go so far as to tell you no feelings are "bad." It's more about how you react and respond to those feelings, but that's a lesson for another day.

Feelings conversations are important because they bring your spouse into the depths of what you are experiencing. We all have feelings, but whether we are willing to identify and express them is what makes the difference. And to be frank, this often takes practice. So many people come from families where feelings conversations did not happen often, if at all. They learned to cover up their feelings, or to stuff them, rather than to express them. In some families, expressing feelings is a sign of weakness rather than a sign of strength. I can't tell you the surprising number of clients I interact with who apologize when they express their emotions by crying in front of me. Emotions are not fickle or weak, and they are not something to apologize for; they are to be recognized, owned, and expressed.

So back to that original conversation. If we're looking to change the response, let's start by changing the question. Instead of just asking "How was your day?" let's dig a little deeper and ask some follow-up questions. "What was the highlight of your day?" "What was the most stressful thing you faced today?" It's important to bring feelings into the conversation by asking our spouse these types of questions and offering up our own feelings.

*Level 4: Beliefs.* No matter what your spiritual background, your underlying beliefs about life, self, and God make up a significant part of who you are. Learning to communicate on this important level is a crucial component to developing an intimate relationship. Conversations of faith and spirituality are a significant part of a couple's connectedness. I know far too many married couples who seem to compartmentalize this part of their life into a box that only comes out at church. But the moment they get back home, it goes back in the box, not to be brought out until next Sunday.

But for those of us who have a relationship with Jesus Christ, this type of conversation should be overflowing from our lives and spilling into every other category. The more we're filled up with Christ, the more He'll begin seeping into our conversations. But we must be deliberate about this process by sitting down with our spouse and making time to pray, read Scripture, discuss Scripture, and share what God is doing in each of our lives. Some of the most intimate times I've had with my husband were not "under the sheets" in our sexual life, but "over the sheets" as we've sat on our bed holding hands, sharing about our walk with God, and praying together—for each other, for our marriage, and for our family. There is nothing more deeply intimate than baring your heart and soul before the Lord with your spouse by your side. Don't take for granted the power and pleasures of level 4 conversation.

## Weekly Couch Time

*But let's be realistic, Debra. Who has time for this kind of conversation with the demands of life, career, and kids?* I can hear some of you saying that right now. I especially see the face of one of my clients, who said that exact thing to me after one of our sessions. *Who has the time?* So many things are fighting for our attention and pulling us in a million different directions. The kids. The chores. The bills. The activities. The ministries. But this is precisely when we need to decide to either continue making excuses and running the rat race of life or to choose marriage.

If you want change, you must start by changing yourself. Sounds simple, but how many times do we ask and pray for our relationships to change without ever taking a personal step in the direction of change? We continue to do the same things, hoping for different results. But marriage is a cause-and-effect relationship. Even if just one person begins to make changes, there will always be a chain reaction. It might not happen overnight, but in time change breeds more change.

One simple assignment I give to couples struggling to find the time to connect in marriage is simply "couch time." You might have heard this called by different names, but it's the basic idea that you need to carve out a 20- to 30-minute chunk of time at least once a week to sit down and connect with no distractions. No television. No phones. No Netflix. No children. Just husband, wife, and a couch. Take it seriously, and schedule it into your calendars. My husband has an alert on his iPhone that goes off every Sunday night at 9:00 p.m., reminding him it's "couch time." The good news is what started as a weekly 20-minute conversation for John and me has turned into hours of conversation that now also take place on different days of the week (again, usually after the kids are in bed). But no matter how much we've talked, no matter what else is going on in our lives, Sunday night at 9:00 remains intact.

Just a few weeks ago his timer went off while we were driving home from a family road trip to Chicago. The kids were all fast asleep in the car, and we had already been chatting off and on for the last ten hours of the drive. But we took the time to go through our usual couch time questions and conversation, because it's our chance to be deliberate and dig deep with each other in the four levels of conversation.

One thing I will suggest for this time is *not* to use it to discuss problems or conflict. That kind of conversation needs to happen at some point, but if you haven't built a reservoir of positive, meaning-ful conversation, you're not going to have the capacity or energy to engage in proper conflict management. Use this time to discuss the positive things in your marriage, to encourage and build up each other, and to share your lives and hearts.

Now for the hard stuff. If you can't discuss conflict during couch time, when do you discuss the hard things on your minds? Learning to engage in healthy communication means recognizing that there is a time and place for the hard stuff, and recognizing when to tackle the hard stuff is half the battle.

## Rules of Engagement

One of my favorite verses dealing with conflict and communica-tion is James 1:19: "Everyone should be quick to listen, slow to speak and slow to become angry." A lot of wisdom is packed into this lit-tle verse, because it's a reminder that there's a way of interacting and communicating that's going to be beneficial to your relationship, and conversely, a way that's going to be destructive. From my clinical observations, if you break down how the average couple deals with conflict, there's a good chance it's going to be more like this: slow to listen, quick to speak, and quick to become angry. We're all guilty of this at some point, aren't we?

> You won't always remember *what* you fought about, but you will always remember *how* you fought about it.

Sometime close to the two-year mark of our marriage, John and I had our first "big blow-out" fight. You know, those ones you see in the movies when there's a lot of yelling, arguing, and tears. I wish I could tell you what it was about, but frankly, I have no idea, and neither does John. Just this morning we were trying desperately to recall what we had argued about so I could include it in this illustration, but we have no recollection of it. That just goes to show you that, years later, you won't always remember *what* you fought about, but you will always remember *how* you fought about it. Take that little nugget of truth and put it in your pocket. I sure wish I had it back then.

At one point during the yelling, each of us trying to get our point across to the other person, I got so angry I couldn't take it anymore. I needed to get away and blow off some steam. I had so much building up inside that I felt like I was about to explode. We were talking ourselves into circles and making no progress. I grabbed the car keys and heatedly walked out of our apartment.

I didn't go far. It wasn't about where I was going; it was more about the gesture I was making by walking out. And truth be told, it wasn't a mature thing to do. After driving around the block for a little while, I waited for him to call or text me. I longed for him to reach out to me. But he didn't. Eventually, I realized I needed to reach out to him. I was the one who walked out, so I needed to be the one to go back.

We were both feeling isolated from each other, needing the same things from each other. Someone had to take a step in the right direction. So I sent him a text. I don't even remember what I said, but I reached out emotionally, and he immediately reached back. I drove back home, and with emotions under control we sat down and talked through it once again, this time in the James 1:19 kind of way: quick to listen, slow to speak, and slow to become angry. And you know what? It worked. We decided that day that we needed some rules to keep this from ever happening again—rules of engagement. If we were going to argue, we had to learn to argue productively. For starters, we would commit to these rules:

1. Never walk out on the other person.

2. Never leave in the middle of an argument.

3. Always seek a resolution before moving on to the next thing.

These were our personal rules of engagement. They kept us engaged, they kept us connected, and they reminded us that no matter how we were feeling, we both had the same end goals in mind: resolution and reconciliation.

I'm not proud of these big blow-out moments, and as potentially embarrassing as it is to share some of them with you, I do it because I want you to realize that everyone goes through hard moments in marriage. Everyone. In every single marriage. It doesn't matter if you're married to Deb, John, Martha, Joe, Benny, Bill, Stacy, April, or Jack... give it some time, and you will hit these hard moments. It doesn't mean you married the wrong person; it just means you're finally discovering what it's like to be married. Deciding to marry someone else instead isn't going to make your marriage problems go away. Any two human beings put together for life will eventually hit hard moments. Even marriage counselors have hard moments in their marriages. We all hit walls that we must learn to take down, or we decide we've reached a dead end. It's either stop or go. And in every single instance, if we're committed to making marriage work, we need to choose to push through together and break down the walls.

## The Speaker-Listener Technique

During my counseling training many years ago, I was introduced to the Speaker-Listener Technique, which changed my understanding of conflict in marriage, and in turn, changed my own marriage. The Speaker-Listener Technique is part of a series of techniques from PREP, which stands for the Prevention and Relationship Enhancement Program.[4] This program was developed based on 30 years of research that came out of the University of Denver, in which they extensively recorded and then observed the communication and interactions of married couples.[5] After watching hour after hour of communication between these couples, they could note patterns of interactions with both positive and negative communication. Through their observations, they could predict with high efficacy which couples exhibited traits that would lead to staying together and which couples exhibited traits that would eventually lead to divorce. Another pioneer in this field is Dr. John Gottman, who could predict with 90 percent accuracy which couples would eventually divorce simply based on their conflict and communication.[6] Conflict and communication are so much more telling than we realize.

Most married couples say communication and conflict management are the most important things in marriage, but most couples don't communicate well. In my survey of over 1000 married people, over 56 percent reported arguing two to nine times every week. That is a lot of conflict married couples are dealing with on a regular basis. Additionally, approximately half of those 1000 married people self-reported that they don't deal with conflict well. They said rather than expressing their emotions and respectfully listening to each other, they got angry and said things they didn't mean, or stayed quiet and didn't deal with the conflict at all. Either way, conflict is not being dealt with in a healthy way. I don't know about you, but I don't think it's a coincidence that the 50 percent in my survey (people who report negative conflict management) coincides with the 50 percent in the national divorce rate reported by the American Psychological Association.[7] There's something to be learned here.

In comes the Speaker-Listener Technique, which essentially offers couples some rules of engagement to help them interact in a way that promotes understanding. According to the PREP research, the Speaker-Listener tool is reported as the technique that helps couples the most.[8] In the Speaker-Listener Technique, two people are involved—the speaker and the listener. Each person has rules to follow to engage in effective communication. Allow me to summarize this helpful technique with a few of my personal thoughts integrated throughout:[9]

### The General Rules

1. The speaker always has the floor. The PREP approach takes this seriously, and will often give the speaker an object to hold to remind both parties whose turn it is to do the speaking. In my office, I used to use the box of tissues on my desk to give to the speaker as a reminder. Originally, it felt kind of silly to the couple, until they both realized how easy it is to interrupt the speaker. Holding something is a tangible way to see who has the floor and helps you take turns when emotions are running high.

2. Share the floor: Take turns being the speaker. Be deliberate about giving each person an equal opportunity to have the floor. You should each aim to have 50 percent of the talking time and 50 percent of the listening time.

3. Don't try to fix it right now. Remember that this isn't about finding a solution; it's about learning to listen well. Be quick to listen and slow to speak. The time for a solution and problem solving will come later, but you can't get there without listening and understanding first. And often, just by listening, you find the problem gets resolved on its own.

### The Speaker Rules

1. Speak for yourself. When you are the speaker and have the floor, it's time to share how you feel, not what you think the other person did or said that was wrong. Use "I" statements to explain your feelings, like "I was hurt when

you didn't call me." Take this time to express your feelings rather than pass blame or point a finger.

2. Keep it simple. It can be easy to go on and on in a conversation, jumping from one thing to another, but make sure you stay focused and keep it simple so that the listener can easily understand your feelings.

3. Pause for paraphrasing. After your turn, the listener will have to respond by paraphrasing what you said. Make sure you pause and give them a chance to respond. If what they paraphrase isn't accurate to how you feel, correct them in a respectful way and reiterate your feelings.

## The Listener Rules

1. Paraphrase what you hear. As the listener, it's your job to listen and hear what's being said by the speaker. Don't just repeat verbatim what you heard like a parrot, but take the time to really listen and put it into your own words. "It sounds like you felt hurt, as though you were unimportant to me when I didn't call."

2. Don't defend yourself. Whether you agree or disagree with what is being said, the point isn't to defend what you did or didn't do, but to make sure your partner feels heard and affirmed. This isn't about being right; it's about learning to listen with love.

## Additional Rules of Engagement

1. Either of you can call Speaker-Listener time anytime you would like to discuss an issue. Whoever calls it begins as the speaker.

2. The listener can choose to reschedule if it's not an

appropriate time for them to talk, but they must reschedule the conversation within 24 hours. This shows the speaker that you care, but it's just not the best time to discuss the issue. The listener should make sure to go back to the conversation by rescheduling it in the moment. "I'm in the middle of finishing this big project for work, but this is important to me. Let's talk about it first thing tomorrow morning."

3. During the conversation, either one of you can call a pause or stop to reiterate the rules or slow down the conversation if it's beginning to escalate or get heated.

### Tearing Down the Walls

Like any conflict management tool or skill, these rules of engagement from the Speaker-Listener Technique will help a couple learn to interact in a positive way. But they aren't the be-all and end-all. They are one more set of knowledge tools to pull from your toolbox. We still have the choice of whether we'll use them. Each couple must commit to creating and applying their own rules of engagement by being vulnerable, letting down their walls, and choosing to reach for intimacy even when intimacy might feel far away.

There's no wall too high, too strong, or too deep that can't be overcome with love, with effort, and with the help of our mighty God. In life, and in marriage, we will come face-to-face with all sorts of walls that try to keep us from one another and prevent us from experiencing true intimacy. But Psalm 18:29 says it this way: "With my God I can scale a wall." I am choosing to hold on to that verse with my whole heart. I believe we serve a God who has the power to give us what we need to begin the process of tearing down the walls of isolation, denial, withdrawal, displacement, invalidation, fantasy, passive-aggression, and rage. In marriage, we're given the opportunity to destroy our walls and erect altars of intimacy in their place. May our walls begin to fall today.

# REFLECTION QUESTIONS
# FOR MARRIED COUPLES

1. Which walls did you observe in your family of origin?
   Which walls do you tend to erect in your marriage?

   a. The Wall of Isolation

   b. The Wall of Denial

   c. The Wall of Withdrawal

   d. The Wall of Displacement

   e. The Wall of Invalidation

   f. The Wall of Fantasy

   g. The Wall of Passive-Aggression

   h. The Wall of Rage

2. Take some time to engage in level 3 and level 4
   conversation with your spouse by asking and answering
   the following questions:

   a. What is something you're feeling stressed or anxious
      about?

   b. What has been the most exciting or fulfilling part of
      your week?

   c. What is something you're looking forward to?

   d. What are some things God is teaching you right now?

   e. How can I be praying for you?

3. How can you be more deliberate to set aside some couch

time this week? Discuss ways to fit this time into your weekly schedule, and then mark it on the calendar!

4. Read and reflect on James 1:19. Which part of this verse do you tend to struggle with? Take some time to ask God to help you grow in this area.

# REFLECTION QUESTIONS FOR SINGLES

1. Which walls did you observe in your family of origin? Which walls do you tend to erect in your personal relationships with friends and family?

    a. The Wall of Isolation

    b. The Wall of Denial

    c. The Wall of Withdrawal

    d. The Wall of Displacement

    e. The Wall of Invalidation

    f. The Wall of Fantasy

    g. The Wall of Passive-Aggression

    h. The Wall of Rage

2. In your family of origin, which of the four levels of communication were most often expressed? Which were not often expressed? How did your family communication affect your personal ability to communicate?

3. Do you need to practice any of the levels of communication with your close friends and family? How can you be more deliberate in practicing healthy communication with others this week?

4. Read and reflect on James 1:19. Which part of this verse do you tend to struggle with? Take some time to ask God to help you grow in this area.

# Alter That Ego

*From Pride to Humility*

H e's such a *narcissist*."
   I counseled a woman for three years who happened to be married to an incredibly self-absorbed man. With significant emotional disconnect in their marriage, suspicions of infidelity, and an intrusive drinking problem, they were in dire need of marriage counseling. But he would never participate. He wasn't even willing to acknowledge there was a need. In his mind, their marriage was fine, and any problems that arose were the result of things she needed to change, not him. According to him, *she was the problem.* And so for three years she attended marriage therapy by herself, with him showing up every once in a blue moon just to keep tabs on what we were doing. With time and effort, she began to recognize her enabling behaviors and eventually get herself to a better place—with or without him.

You've probably heard the term *narcissist* used to describe someone lately. I've heard that term come up more and more frequently from the different men and women I've interacted with or counseled over the years—whether from a wife complaining about her husband, someone venting about their child or coworker, or even journalists on television referring to some politicians. It's a word that's becoming more and more popular and even part of everyday lingo. In case you don't know the background for this term, let me tell you the story from which it originates.

There's a tale in Greek mythology about a figure named Narcissus who was extremely handsome. He was so incredibly good-looking that many people fell in love with him. But instead of accepting their love, in his arrogance and pride, he felt disdain toward them. He was too good for anyone and everyone. Then one day, Narcissus came upon a pool of water and went to get a drink. As he leaned over, he noticed his reflection looking back at him. He became so infatuated with the image of himself that he could not leave his reflection, and eventually died there, alone in his sorrow.

This mythological story of Narcissus has shaped much of what we think and believe about the problem of pride. In modern psychiatry, an actual personality disorder is named after this mythological character: narcissistic personality disorder. The official *Diagnostic and Statistical Manual of Mental Disorders* counselors and psychologists use to diagnose mental illness (DSM-V) has an entire category identifying the features of narcissistic personality disorder.[1] And while so many of us might be quick to throw around the term *narcissist* to describe people in our lives, true narcissistic personality disorder is a rare occurrence, diagnosed in less than 6 percent of the general population, with 50 to 75 percent of those who receive the diagnosis male (no offense, guys, just stating the statistics here).[2]

But as I read through the description of this personality disorder, I can't help but notice some disturbingly familiar terms catching my eye within the diagnostic criteria:

- Exaggerated self-appraisal

- Sees oneself as exceptional

- Sense of entitlement

- Lack of empathy
- Impaired ability to recognize the feelings and needs of others
- Little interest in other's experiences
- Self-centeredness
- Belief that one is better than others
- Condescending toward others
- Admiration seeking

I don't know about you, but as I read through this list, I have to admit that at different points in my life I've identified with every single one of those pesky little traits. Whether or not we admit it, and whether or not we've reached the extreme, there's a little bit of Narcissus in each and every one of us. Moments when we believe we're better than the rest. Moments when we feel we can't possibly be wrong. Moments when we're so caught up with our emotions and needs that we can't even begin to fathom the feelings and needs of others. Moments when we desperately long for attention and admiration. Whether it's extreme or subtle, we all carry a little bit of Narcissus inside of us. We just call him by another name: pride.

## Pride Comes Before the Fall

Pride absolutely cannot be ignored. God's Word refers to the negative trait of pride in 61 different texts throughout the Old and New Testaments.[3] It's used to describe a general arrogant attitude toward others but also refers to a series of inconsiderate actions and behaviors. The most interesting thing about the presence of pride is that most often it is followed by destruction, downfall, disgrace, deceit, and even death.

- *Destruction:* Pride is the first step toward destruction. Proud thoughts will lead you to defeat (Proverbs 16:18 ERV).

- *Downfall:* But when his heart and mind were puffed up with arrogance, he was brought down from his royal throne and stripped of his glory (Daniel 5:20 NLT).

- *Disgrace:* When pride comes, then comes disgrace, but with humility comes wisdom (Proverbs 11:2).

- *Deceit:* The terror you inspire and the pride of your heart have deceived you (Jeremiah 49:16).

- *Death:* But when Uzziah became strong, his pride caused him to be destroyed. He was not faithful to the LORD his God (2 Chronicles 26:16 ERV). (Later in this passage, we find it was Uzziah's prideful actions that ultimately caused him to be inflicted with leprosy and die a slow, painful death.)

Scripture's warning about pride is as loud and clear as a fire alarm ringing from a burning building. To ignore or deny its presence would be to consider yourself an absolute fool, because "pride goes before destruction, a haughty spirit before a fall" (Proverbs 16:18). But many times pride subtly creeps into our lives without our realizing it's there; without acknowledging its presence, without calling it out for what it us. We live with it in our lives, in our relationships, and in our marriages until it slowly begins to do some major damage, eroding the foundation of our relationships. It affects our ability to feel a positive emotional connection to the people around us ("*Look at all their flaws*"), it influences our desire to understand the feelings and needs of others ("*They are the problem*"), and more alarming, it makes an impact on our ability to see where we've been wrong ("*This isn't my fault*").

Pride is the number-one thing that negatively influences arguments, conflict, and tension in a relationship, because "where there is strife, there is pride" (Proverbs 13:10). The two will always go hand in hand.

## "Chocolate" Humble Pie

My husband sinned against me.

Seriously, he did.

I was having a rough day, and I opened my top-secret drawer where I hide my desperate-times-call-for-desperate-measures chocolate stash. It was missing! *My chocolate stash was missing.* The stash I cling to in case of emergencies. The stash I spend a little extra money on just to have, knowing that I'll use it wisely and savor it piece by piece. The no-kids-allowed, husband-stay-away, one-and-only-stinking-thing-in-life-I-call-my-very-own stash. And immediately (considering the location of this particular stash and the fact that it was only known by the two of us) I knew it had to be my husband who broke into it.

*He knows this is my secret stash. He promised not to touch it. He didn't even tell me about it! I'll bet he didn't even savor it! He probably finished it all in all of 30 seconds. Can he be trusted? Does he even love me?*

Okay, call me a bit dramatic, but I was seriously fuming. Maybe it sounds like such a small thing to you, but anyone who is married knows it's usually not the big things that tend to cause a marital rift. Most often, it's the small things. And you know what? This wasn't even about the chocolate anymore. It was about the principle! It was about the trust. It was about him keeping his word and respecting my boundaries. I was annoyed. I was mad. But more than that, or should I say, *underneath all that*, I was hurt.

A few minutes later my daughter, who was four at the time, walked into our room while we were discussing "the situation." We make it a priority to be wise about what we discuss around our children, but she overheard the part about the chocolate. "It's okay, Mommy. You can share your chocolate with all of us!" she said with a beaming smile. Let me put it out there: it's a humbling moment when your four-year-old models more grace and forgiveness than you do. Talk about getting served a nice big slice of "chocolate" humble pie. But the bottom line is this wasn't just about sharing; it was about choosing to respond with love when I had every "right" to be annoyed, frustrated, and hurt. It was about seeking an attitude of reconciliation rather than sitting on the throne of condescendence.

It was about letting go of my pride (*You're the problem. I'm hurt. This is all about me. I have done no wrong here*) and instead learning to move forward with humility, grace, and forgiveness (*Do I have a responsibility or role in this? I'm not perfect either. How can we resolve this and come together? Could I be misinterpreting this? How can this be used as an opportunity for grace?*).

## It's a Humility Thing

I've found that one of the best ways to measure how humble we are is to look at how quick we are to forgive. Forgiveness requires us to lay down what may be *rightfully* ours (our hurts, our grievances, our desire to seek revenge) in exchange for something greater (healing, peace, and reconciliation). But sometimes our pride gets in the way of making that important exchange because it completely blinds us to our own flaws and weaknesses. Have you ever been in a rush to head out the door when you realize you've lost your keys? Or your glasses? Or your wallet? Or a shoe? (Yep, that last one happens to me far more often than I'd like to admit.) I tend to be an organized person, but with three kids, it's not uncommon to find me running around the house desperately looking for something minutes before we need to leave. I go into crazy-panicked-lady mode, thinking of the most obscure places I might be able to find that lost thing. But you know what's even worse than losing something you need two seconds before you head out the door? *Finding it a half hour later in the most obvious place!* I promise you, I've often thoroughly looked for something in a certain spot twice, only to somehow magically find it right in front of my face the third time. It drives me absolutely mad!

It can be so easy to miss something that is right in front of our eyes. Not only do we do this with our *things*, but we do it with our *selves* too. In the heat of an argument or disagreement, or in the face of an offense, it's easy to focus on the faults of the other person and completely overlook our own. If we're not careful, we see what we want to see rather than what's really there. And in our oblivion, we magnify the flaws of others while minimizing or missing our own.

In the book of Matthew, Jesus says we're so quick to look at the speck in another's eye while ignoring the gigantic plank in our eye (Matthew 7:3). What an accurate picture of our tendency to exaggerate the flaws of others. To let go of our faulty perspective, we've got to first get a glimpse of truth. We've got to let go of the false idea of who we think we are and open our eyes to the reality of who we actually are—sinners in need of Christ's mercy. When we see God, others, and ourselves accurately, we'll have a much easier time letting go of our pride and choosing humility instead. We've got to get to a point where we can say no to flesh (what *I* would rather say and do) and yes to Spirit (what *God* is calling me to say and do).

I've really come to terms with the importance of this necessary introspection, because if I'm honest, it's something I wrestle with daily. Not only am I quick to point out the flaws I see in others (namely, my dear husband), but I'm also the type of person who finds it hard to forgive when I've been wronged because I want the person who has hurt me to know just how hurt I really am. And because, frankly, sometimes sulking feels downright *good*, doesn't it? But as we all know, the longer we hold on to wrongs, the faster the seeds of bitterness and contempt begin to take root in our hearts, ultimately suffocating our relationships with the poison of pride. For a relationship to have any hope of thriving, we need to learn to let go of our pride in exchange for something greater—humility.

## Choosing Humility

But let's be practical. It's not always easy to say no to your flesh and yes to your spirit when you're fuming mad. How do you get over the fact that you don't even like your spouse in the moment, much less move into the act of loving your spouse? How do you let go of the hurt, the pain, and the pride holding you back to reach for an attitude of humility? Having been married for over a decade, I can assure you that I've had a lot of practice in dealing with my pride. In the early years of our marriage, I tended to sit with my pride and deal with strife for much longer than I should have. Thankfully, John and I established a rule early in our marriage that we would take Ephesians 4:26 literally—"Do not let the sun go down while you are still angry"—and never allow ourselves to go to bed harboring any conflict. Many nights we'd simply extend our bedtime because neither of us was ready to let go of our pride and move forward in humility and love! But over the years, God has used the beautiful, sanctifying work of marriage to mold us, to change us, and to transform us. We're much quicker at "altering our ego" and moving toward reconciliation rather than holding on to strife through the wee hours of the morning.

## Alter Your Ego

I'm not naive enough to think stolen chocolate is at the height of all marital strife and conflict. But as I said earlier, often the small things of life cause more conflict than the big things. In my survey of over 1000 married people, 72 percent reported it's not the big things, like infidelity, addictions, abuse, or sexual struggles, that tend to cause hardships in their marriage. It's the daily, little things, like dealing with conflict and tension and balancing work, children, and chores.

No matter who you are reading this book, or whether you are single or married, I can assure you a time will come when you are feeling stuck in your ability to respond to someone you love. It can be hard to let go of our ego and move from pride to humility and from hurt to forgiveness when our flesh is kicking and screaming! But over the years, three things have helped me overcome the hurdle of self and learn to choose *we* over *me*. I share them with my clients, but I want to also share them with you.

*I think of who God is:* I'll never forget the moment when I first discovered this little trick. I look back and know it was a Holy Spirit thing, because God knew I would need this lesson time and time again in so many parts of my life. It was early in our marriage, and I was feeling so hurt and frustrated about who-knows-what-now. I remember escaping to our bedroom after a heated discussion. And as I was alone in our room, I heard God's voice speaking to my heart so clearly. *Think of Me...think of all that I've done for you. And then, respond...not to your husband, but to My love for you.* And so I spent the next few minutes meditating on who God was in my life and how much He had forgiven me from. I thought about my many sins in comparison to God's ocean of grace and love and mercy.

In light of my sins and grievances toward Him, God has every right to retaliate, to distance, to separate from me. But instead He chose to lay that all down for me. In those moments, alone in my room, my heart began to quickly melt. I needed to respond to who God was by showing my husband the same kind of love, even if I felt it was undeserved. Because, really, who of us is deserving?

Thinking about the glorious, breathtaking character of my God still reminds me that I want to be more like Him and less like me. And that reality almost always melts my ice-cold heart.

*I think of who my spouse is:* One Valentine's Day (which is also my hubby's birthday) I made John a picture-framed image of a heart made of words. Each sentence in the heart explained something I love about him. "I *love*...the way you smile so huge when you're getting to the good part of the movie...your tenderness in loving me...that you play tag with the kids even after a long day's work when I know you're exhausted...your perfectly soft hands...how proud you are of me...the passion you have for your job...how talented you are at finding an excellent bargain...your voice...that you're so responsible with your time...how you prioritize our family..." The list of more than 100 things went on and on—small things, silly things, significant things, all wrapped up into a glimpse of who my husband is.

I come back to this list often, whether in a tangible way, by picking it up and looking over it, or just in my imagination. I keep a place in my mind and my heart where I remember who my husband really is. And in those moments when I am hurt or annoyed or frustrated, I try to remember who it is I married and what I love most about him. I married a good man, and even on those days when I am feeling hurt, I choose to remember that his mistakes aren't what define him, but rather, his heart.

Who of us would ever want to be defined by our mistakes? Whether you are dealing with something big or small, it's important to take a step back and remember that your identity is not wrapped up in the choices you make in the moment (whether bad or good). Your identity is so much deeper than that, because it's wrapped up in a God who sees your value apart from anything you do or say.

That's not to say there's no accountability for our actions, because there will always be consequences for our mistakes here on this earth. Consequences are part of the healing process and move us toward a place of change. But as individuals and as spouses, we have a choice to make: fixate on the negatives and brood with bitterness or remember the positives and have a balanced perspective as we deal with our hurts and grievances. That list is a helpful reminder for me to keep the negatives in check by focusing on the positives.

*I think of who I am:* Pride deceives us into thinking we're better than others. It minimizes our weaknesses and fools us into believing we're not the type of people who could make "those kinds" of mistakes. That faulty perspective can quickly bring us to a place where we're looking down on the people closest to us. The apostle Paul said it like this to the people of Rome: "Do not think of yourself more highly than you ought, but rather think of yourself with sober judgment" (Romans 12:3). Take that phrase in for a moment—*sober judgment.* When we've been hurt, we tend to act and think in un-sober-like ways.

We can get so "drunk" with hurt and anger that our view of ourselves becomes irrationally better than it ought to be.

Humility asks us to keep ourselves in check by remembering that we are all sinners in need of major grace. In the book of Hosea, God's holy prophet was asked to marry Gomer, a woman who would ultimately engage in a life of unfaithfulness and infidelity. Time and time again, she would leave the safety of unconditional love to seek out momentary pleasures and sin. And time and time again, Hosea would welcome her back with outstretched arms.

If I'm totally real with you here, as a therapist, I find myself reading through that story and thinking, *That is the most toxic relationship ever*. But this story isn't a model for our relationships, because this story is about so much more than Hosea and Gomer. This story is God's way of reminding His people that this type of toxicity is also found in every single one of us. We are so quick to leave the safety of the unconditional love of God to seek out momentary pleasures. As the old hymn puts it so well, we are people "prone to wander, Lord I feel it. Prone to leave the God I love."[4] The realization that we are just as capable of wrongdoing as everyone else has the power to not only increase our love for God, but heighten our grace for others. When I find myself struggling to forgive, I have to take a step back and think of who I am, remembering that I am a person in constant need of forgiveness from a God who takes me back time and time again. Only then am I enabled to extend the same grace to others. "Be kind and compassionate to one another, forgiving each other, just as in Christ God forgave you" (Ephesians 4:32).

## Forgiveness Is for You

For every single wound that life throws at us, there also comes a parallel need for forgiveness; the need to heal from the past, live in the present, and move into the future. And not for the sake of the person who hurt us, but for ourselves. Holding on to hurts means holding on to the past, and holding on to the past will always keep us from moving forward. Oftentimes we wait for an apology, wait for remorse, or wait for reconciliation. But when we wait for those who have hurt us to change, we end up wasting our lives away, putting control in their hands instead of our own.

God challenges us to move into forgiveness because it's the only way we begin to take back control and live our lives again. But please don't ever mistake forgiveness for forgetting. Forgiveness doesn't mean you ignore harmful behaviors. And forgiveness doesn't mean you continue to allow unhealthy patterns without enforcing consequences and boundaries. Forgiveness isn't given because you're okay with what happened. But forgiveness *does* mean moving forward. It means letting go of whatever is holding you back. It means giving yourself the opportunity to heal. It means allowing yourself the necessary steps toward change. At the end of the day, forgiveness isn't for the person who hurt you. It's for you. It's for you to be free. To move on. To take the next steps. Forgiveness is for you, from a loving God who knows exactly what's best for your life: *freedom.*

●——●

So whatever came of the chocolate ordeal, you ask? Well, after I settled down, and after my husband stopped feeling defensive, we sat and talked. Not about chocolate, but about what was really going on beneath the surface. About expectations, selflessness, boundaries, and trust. About what I needed from him, and what he needed from me. We confessed, we apologized, we took responsibility, we forgave, and we met each other right there in the middle. We showed each other love. It was a beautiful moment for us, a moment I'll cherish for a long time.

And the grace and forgiveness we learned to bestow on each other in the small things are the very same grace and forgiveness that have carried us through the harder things. Countless times John and I have had to let go of our pride in exchange for humility as we've practiced forgiveness in the face of sins big and small. We've had our fair share of difficult moments in marriage. Because like it or not, it's not *if* you will sin against each other; it's *when* you'll sin against each other—and, more importantly, *how* you'll choose to move forward from that point on. But each of those moments has offered us the invitation to deepen our love, strengthen our communication, and solidify our commitment to each other. Each of those moments has allowed us the incredible responsibility and privilege of choosing marriage—the hardest and greatest thing you'll ever do.

To anyone else out there who's struggled to "like" their spouse, for big reasons or small, may we always remember that a good marriage isn't about bypassing arguments, hurts, and struggles, but about learning to lean into those things with love. And inevitably, when we choose to love we'll often find that we get "like" thrown in shortly thereafter, no matter which side of the apology we're on.

## The Art of Apology

Earlier I mentioned that a good gauge of how humble you are is to look at how quick you are to forgive. But did you know pride and humility are also displayed in another important interpersonal skill? Apology. And believe it or not, very few people ever learn how to apologize.

From early on in childhood, we're taught that to apologize is to say "Sorry." You probably remember a time when a friend or sibling was forced to apologize to you, or a time when you were forced to apologize to someone. I don't know about you in childhood, but my kids have pretty much mastered the unapologetic apology. On nearly a daily basis, one of them is asked to apologize to the other(s) for something they did that was rude or inconsiderate. Just today I asked Eli (my five-year-old son) to apologize to Ella (my soon-to-be seven-year-old girl) for continually spraying her with the hose outside even after she asked him repeatedly not to do so. "I'm sowwy, Ewwa," he said with his cutest little pouty voice. But then within moments he did it again. Call me crazy, but something about that gesture confirmed to me that he wasn't truly sorry.

In many instances in childhood, and then on through adulthood, we tend to hold on to the belief that to give an apology is to simply spout out the word *sorry*. Worse yet, we can often give an apology with our lips, while our hearts are far from being apologetic. But if the true definition of an apology is a regretful acknowledgment of one's offense or failure, then the words "I'm sorry" do very little in conveying an apologetic heart. If we want to master the art of apology, we've got to really break it down into simple, but very important steps.

### Step 1: Acknowledge What You Are Sorry For

When it comes to a meaningful apology, it's important to start with what it is you're sorry for. What did you do that led to the conflict, strife, or hurt feelings? It might seem like a no-brainer to say it out loud, but confessing your wrongdoing not only signifies that you're taking responsibility for your actions and your contribution to the problem, but also ensures that you and your partner are both on the same page. It's also important to avoid vague terminology, and instead be specific about what it is you regret doing. For example, "I'm sorry I used a rude tone with you" or "I apologize that I didn't take you into consideration when I made plans."

### Step 2: Explain Why It Was Hurtful

After you acknowledge what you did, you've got to move into how it affected the person standing before you. This is where it's important to acknowledge the hurt feelings that resulted from your behavior. It helps your partner know that you get where they are coming from and why they are hurt. "I'm sorry I didn't take you into consideration when I made plans. It was wrong because it made you feel like you weren't important to me." Acknowledging the feelings behind the conflict is one of the most important conflict resolution skills a counselor will teach you in marriage or premarriage therapy. Don't underestimate the importance of affirming your spouse's emotions. Sometimes that affirmation alone is what moves the conversation to a better place.

### Step 3: Express *How You Plan on Moving Forward*

This is the part where an apology moves from simple words into action. A sincere apology not only acknowledges what has been done and explains why it was hurtful, but then expresses what is going to happen to keep it from happening in the future. I once heard it said that a sincere apology means from now on you're going to do things differently. So how are you going to move forward to assure your spouse that you care enough to prevent this from happening again? "I'm sorry I didn't take you into consideration when I made plans. It was wrong because it made you feel like you weren't important. From now on, I promise to discuss plans with you and ask for your feedback before I make these kinds of decisions."

### Step 4: Ask for Forgiveness

The last part to the apology is the simplest, yet the most humbling. Once you've acknowledged what you did, explained why it was hurtful, and expressed how you're moving forward, it's time to ask for forgiveness. *Will you forgive me?* A few simple words have the power to convey your desire to reconcile, reconnect, and move forward together.

## The Power of Humility

Whether we're the one who was wrong or the one who was wronged, both ends of the spectrum require an exchange to occur in our heart: from pride to humility. It takes as much humility to accept an apology and offer forgiveness as it does to give an apology and receive forgiveness. Humility has the power to bring two people together in a way that not many other things can manage to do. A 2015 study examined the role of humility in the context of romantic relationships and concluded that couples who perceived a higher level of humility in their partners also had a higher level of commitment, trust, forgiveness, and an overall increase in relationship satisfaction.[5] Isn't it amazing how we can look to research to tell us exactly what God's Word has already made clear? There is a direct positive correlation between the presence of humility and the health and satisfaction of our relationships.

- Be completely humble and gentle; be patient, bearing with one another in love (Ephesians 4:2).

- As God's chosen people, holy and dearly loved, clothe yourselves with compassion, kindness, humility, gentleness and patience (Colossians 3:12).

- Be like-minded, be sympathetic, love one another, be compassionate and humble (1 Peter 3:8).

- Clothe yourselves with humility toward one another (1 Peter 5:5).

God's principles are timeless. His plans for marriage and relationships make so much sense, because He is the one and only being who knows the intricacies behind what makes them work. As we take inventory of our ego, may we be challenged to let go of every ounce of pride that might be getting in the way and exchange it for a heart of humility.

Because marriage has the power to shed our ego, the real question is this: will we allow it to?

## REFLECTION QUESTIONS
## FOR MARRIED COUPLES

1. Proverbs 13:10 reminds us that "where there is strife, there is pride." In what specific ways does pride tend to affect your marriage?

2. Think about a recent time of conflict. What could you have done differently to contribute to a better outcome? How could you apply the steps toward forgiveness or the art of apology to that situation? Take some time to practice taking responsibility for your part of the conflict by discussing it with your spouse.

3. Is your tendency to struggle with forgiving well or apologizing well? What steps can you take to start changing your pattern for the future?

4. Are you currently harboring any bitterness or lack of forgiveness in your marriage? What are some steps you can take toward healing?

## REFLECTION QUESTIONS
## FOR SINGLES

1. Read Matthew 7:3. What are the negative actions, words, or behaviors you tend to display when you're upset? How can you take responsibility for your role in conflict?

2. Does anyone come to mind toward whom you are currently "holding a grudge"? What are some steps you need to take toward forgiveness and healing?

3. Is your tendency to struggle with forgiving well or apologizing well? What steps can you take to start changing your pattern for the future?

# 5

# The Struggle Is Real

*From Expectations to Reality*

The expectations were high that evening. My husband and I had planned a much-needed date night shortly after the birth of our third child. It had been an unusually stressful year for us, and we were both in major need of some alone time, tasty food, and great conversation. We were looking forward to unplugging from life and connecting with each other over a nice meal. Someone had suggested this great local restaurant, and we were looking forward to trying it out. We'd heard wonderful things about it from different people, so we arrived hungry, ready to down some good food.

I don't know if we caught them on an off day, or if there was some sort of a full moon, because every single thing we ordered turned out seriously disappointing. Strike one: the buffalo chicken wing appetizers were burned to a blackened crisp. They tasted about as "buffalo-flavored" as a forest fire. Strike two: I found a hair in my sandwich. Enough said. Strike three: the guacamole topping on one of our entrees was as dark as a layer of tar. I'm pretty sure I remembered guacamole being green. I don't know about you, but for us, three strikes were about all we could handle. We asked for our bill and couldn't wait to get outta there.

The manager noticed the plethora of mistakes and kindly came over to let us know that our bill would be covered, and handed us a gift card to come back and give them another chance. I don't think we'll take them up on the offer, but it was certainly a kind gesture.

I think what made this date-night dinner experience so disappointing wasn't simply the poor quality of the restaurant's food (though that didn't help), but the high expectations we had going into the dinner. You know what I mean, right? It's like that amazing movie everyone's been talking about nonstop, and then you finally sit down and watch it and realize it's not as great as you had hoped. Or that vacation you were so desperately looking forward to, imagining how perfect it would be while sitting there in your cubicle at work. And then something (or everything?) goes wrong. The weather decides to rain on you. Flights get delayed or canceled. Or the kids get a terrible case of strep throat the day before you leave for Disney (yep, that's a true story too, but I'll save it for another day).

Sometimes our high expectations end up being the very things that let us down. We want something so badly that we'd rather hold on tightly to our unrealistic expectations than prepare for reality. Too many people have a similar view when it comes to marriage. They have such high hopes of what it will be like that they never take the time to prepare for reality. Then when reality hits they're left with major disappointments, deep hurts, and shattered dreams.

## We Didn't Think It Would Be This Hard

Candice said she and her husband, Darrell, were like two ships passing in the night, floating on dark and stormy waters. They had been married for almost four years, and to put it bluntly, this was definitely not what they thought marriage would be like. According to Candice, they thought marriage would be a lot like dating—plenty of date nights, limited disagreements, romantic dinners out, and lots of fun. But then real life hit. The romantic dinners got replaced by bills, and the date nights got replaced by a crying infant who kept them up throughout the night. "I expected our relationship to exist in some sort of a vacuum. I felt like the outside forces of the world wouldn't affect the two of us," Candice shared.

They were both very laid-back people, and the thought of peacefully coasting through life together didn't sound like a far-reaching scenario. But just a short while into it, "marriage got hard." They realized the expectation of marriage and the reality of marriage were two very different things. With a new baby, crazy hours at work, and financial stressors piling up, physical and emotional exhaustion quickly set in and began to affect their relationship. They both felt tired and burned out. They were irritable and tense. "Expectations were at an all-time high, but we were both shooting very low, not quite living up to the high standards we set for each other," Candice explained. "I didn't think marriage would be this hard, because in reality the easy part is committing your life to someone in front of hundreds of people. The hard part comes two weeks later, when you actually have to follow through on your promise to love someone more than you love yourself for the rest of your life."

I know for certain that many people are navigating through the struggles of unmet and unrealistic expectations in marriage. Not only have I seen it played out in my own marriage, but I've witnessed it in the couples I counsel and in the married friends I interact with along the way. I'd go so far as to say every couple experiences this somewhere along the journey of marriage. It's something everyone goes through, yet no one talks about. We often go so far as to keep it hidden. I can't tell you how many private messages and emails I get from friends and acquaintances who've reached the end of their rope, desperately asking for marriage advice because "this is not what I thought it would be like." But the most interesting thing about this, and what makes me realize how prominent this feeling is, is that almost always the people reaching out to me are people you would never guess are struggling in their marriages.

I remember one day a former classmate of mine posted a beautiful tribute to her husband on their anniversary. Reading her words brought tears to my eyes because they were just so eloquently written and seemingly heartfelt. But within hours, I received an unexpected, heartbreaking message in my inbox, informing me they were on the brink of divorce and needed help. Dealing with addictions, broken trust, and the overwhelming demands of life, they didn't know where to turn. This isn't what they thought marriage would be like.

I think we can all identify with the truth that our expectations are often not in line with the reality of marriage. And until we get our expectations right, we're going to live a disappointed life. But if we could change the way we think about marriage, recognizing our assumptions and replacing them with truth, we could truly begin to enjoy the blessings marriage has to offer. And if you're single and reading this, I hope you're paying close attention, because getting this stuff right *before* marriage has the power to completely revolutionize the way you do relationships.

## What Did I Expect?

I had a set of flowery expectations going into marriage. I was in my early twenties when I first met John, and I was completely enamored with the love of my life and soon-to-be husband. He could absolutely do no wrong in my eyes (and I'll be honest—neither could I)! We had a healthy dating relationship, and since dating was perpetually awesome, naturally I assumed marriage would be even more awesome. Why wouldn't it be?

I'll never forget the conversation we had with our pastor during our premarriage counseling sessions. We had just filled out an assessment unpacking our expectations in marriage. The pastor we were meeting with (who also happened to be a licensed professional counselor) sat us down, looked at me with sincere eyes, and said, "Debra, according to this assessment, you seem to have really idealistic expectations for this relationship." And he was right. In looking through my answers, I had pretty much decided that my husband-to-be was amazing in every possible way. He could do no wrong and would do no wrong. My levels of satisfaction were through the roof, and I assumed they would always be that way! After reviewing my answers, we spent some time discussing the reality of marriage and what we could expect along the way.

> You can't experience real love with a person until you've experienced the entirety of a person.

It's funny looking back at that assessment, because I would answer those questions differently now. After ten years of marriage, I see John in a much deeper, more significant way. He's no longer the husband-who-could-do-no-wrong-and-would-do-no-wrong. Rather, he's a human being who has flaws, weaknesses, and sins, just like I do. I've seen the beautiful sides to him, and I've also seen the ugly sides to him. Sides he's also seen in me. But even though my answers would be different today, my love for him is also so much more significant. What makes marriage so incredible is that even in the reality of who he is, my love for him is so much deeper. Not despite his weaknesses, but *because* of his weaknesses. I see him, the real him, and I love him more deeply with each day. You can't experience real love with a person until you've experienced the entirety of a person—the good, the bad, the ugly, and the beautiful.

## From Assumptions to Truth

We all enter relationships with a set of underlying assumptions, even though we often don't notice their existence. They shape our actions, choices, behaviors, and feelings, and they influence our interactions. But where do these assumptions come from? Believe it or not, we cultivate our assumptions and expectations through the many different relationships we experience. Our view of relationships is shaped by the relationships we engage in starting from the earliest years of our life. Everything we know about love begins taking shape based on how love was communicated to us in the early years of our childhood within the context of our family of origin. Assumptions are shaped by past relationship experiences, from the way we interacted with our parents or the people who raised us, to the friendships we develop, to the people we date, and all the way through to marriage. And slowly, those assumptions begin making their way into how we interact with the people closest to us, which is oftentimes why they go unnoticed until we get married.

In a survey of over 1000 married people, I asked them to identify what area of marriage came with the biggest reality check, meaning their expectations for how they would navigate these areas turned out to be much harder in reality. Starting with the most common, here's what they reported.

## Finances (24.4%)

You're probably not surprised by this answer, because we all hear the phrase "financial stress is one of the leading causes of divorce" thrown around. Our view of money and spending comes down to an assumption we bring with us into marriage. Whether we're wired to spend, or to save, or somewhere in between, what we've learned about finances is directly influenced by what we've witnessed. Differences in assumptions can cause some serious stress in a relationship.

I met with a young man who was in the process of uncovering how his views of money were starting to affect his relationship. Growing up in a home where there was financial instability and strain, he came to be a firm believer in working hard and saving wisely. His girlfriend, though, was on the opposite side of the spending spectrum.

She wanted to enjoy life by spending along the way. As you can imagine, these differences in financial assumptions and beliefs were going to eventually work their way into the reality check of their future marriage. I was proud to see two people who could identify and begin working through these assumptions before they entered marriage.

On the other side of the financial spectrum, I met a married couple in the middle of the struggle because neither of them were savers. They both had a casual view of money and spent their way through their weekly paychecks. Coming from families where money was never really discussed, neither of them had ever learned to budget, plan, or save. It was only a few years into marriage and after having children that the topics of debt, money, and spending became a huge burden in their marriage. It was causing stress, tension, and a major rift in their relationship. The assumptions they had unknowingly carried about money were now directly influencing their marriage.

If you find yourself struggling with this aspect of marriage, it's time for a reality check. Do yourself and your marriage a favor and pick up a copy of the book *Dave Ramsey's Complete Guide to Money*. Start applying principles that will help you make wise financial choices before your choices begin to make you.

### Lifestyle Differences (19.7%)

I was somewhat surprised that this answer came in so high on the list because John and I rarely deal with lifestyle differences in our marriage. But it just goes to show you that every couple has their unique set of challenges. My husband and I are pretty similar in our lifestyle choices and standard of living. We like the same foods, enjoy the same hobbies, practice the same faith, come from the same cultural background, prioritize the same values, enjoy the same vacations, have similar ways of doing things around the house, and have common beliefs and opinions about most things big and small. Except for this one thing—our *social* lifestyles.

I came from a family that was all about socializing. Everything we did—from holidays, to parties, to family dinners—involved lots and lots of people. There were people at my home pretty much every hour of every day. It was commonplace to have additional settings at our dinner table because someone extra would always be invited, whether a friend, a neighbor, or a missionary or church leader passing through who needed a place to stay. Family gatherings like Christmas and Thanksgiving involved at least 50 to 100 people, and there was always the guarantee of two things: tons of noise and a whole lot of good food.

I remember my first holiday experiences with John's family shortly after we first got married, because they were probably the first times my expectations of marriage were met with the reality of marriage. Sitting around the quiet Thanksgiving table with just a handful of immediate family was totally not what I was used to. At my Thanksgiving celebrations, there is no such thing as quiet, or dining room tables for that matter—just one long, loud, and crazy buffet line. Thanksgiving with the Filetas was quiet, intimate, and more relaxed than anything I'd ever experienced.

If I'm honest, I have to admit it was hard for me to adjust during those first few years of marriage. It almost felt as though I was "missing something" in being away from my big, fat, loud Egyptian family. I remember escaping upstairs during our first holiday together as a married couple and letting out a few tears in the middle of a lifestyle difference I was learning to adapt to.

No matter what aspect of lifestyle we're talking about (social life, hobbies, preferences, activity levels, timeliness, cleanliness, and so on), these differences can easily cause hardships in a relationship because of the nature of two different people learning to become one. But then again, they also have the power to connect two people in an intimate way. Even in the places where we've experienced lifestyle differences, we've learned to accommodate and learn from each other. Believe it or not, in this area, I've learned to let go of my assumption that "my way of doing life is better" and have seen the importance of focused, committed, intimate family time as a direct result of being married to John. He's taught me how to slow down and soak in life. When it comes to our personal social lifestyles, John and I have learned to see the extremes of the different families we come from, and have decided to create a *new* family culture with a balance of social time and family time that works for us.

### Sexual Issues (18.4%)

Sexual struggles are so common in marriage, yet sadly, rarely talked about. And I can wrap my brain around why that is. For most Christians, it's not the most comfortable topic of discussion to begin with. Add to that, it's a topic that's unfortunately not often addressed or taught about in the church at large. But it's such an important aspect of marriage because we carry mountains of assumptions and expectations going into sex. No one really thinks about sexual issues before they get married because, let's get real, it's hard to keep your hands off each other in anticipation of that wedding night, much less think through the different struggles you might face in your sexual relationship.

I've committed an entire chapter to the topic of sexual intimacy in marriage a little later in this book, but it's important to acknowledge that it's an area the typical couple doesn't know enough about going into marriage. I mean, seriously, how much "research" does the average person do about how to engage and maintain a healthy sexual life? To be frank, I don't think John or I ever thought about the concept of "sexual issues" before marriage, because we were so busy thinking about how great sex would be when we finally got married.

Some of these topics didn't even come to mind for me until I was in my graduate program for counseling, and even then, not until I began to see couples in my counseling office for sexual issues. I remember one of the very first times I worked with a couple who came in for sexual issues. They had been married for four years and hadn't consummated their marriage—meaning, they hadn't had sex. After a series of counseling sessions, we were able to dig deep and uncover the impact both of their pasts had on shaping their current sexual experience, as well as the underlying assumptions about sex and sexuality they each had carried into marriage. There was a lot of guilt and shame attached to the topic of sex, and those assumptions had to be undone through the process of counseling. The good news is that within just a few months of counseling, they were slowly but surely able to move forward in healing and finally experience sexual intercourse. But what's interesting to note here is that these types of sexual struggles aren't as uncommon as one would think—they just aren't talked about. I mean, it's not the kind of conversation a person has over a caramel latte while sitting at Starbucks (but maybe it should be)!

So many people are dealing with the reality check of sexual issues, and unfortunately, because of the stigma we've created surrounding this important topic, they end up needlessly suffering for far too long. Now that we've put it out there that sexual issues are commonplace in marriage, my prayer is that those of you who are experiencing such struggles will find in this book comfort and encouragement to seek the help of a professional counselor. No matter what aspect of sexual struggles you're experiencing in your marriage, there's always hope for healing. Like I said, much more on this is coming up later, in chapter 8. And for another remarkable resource on sex in marriage, pick up a copy of the book *Sheet Music* by Dr. Kevin Leman.

### Dealing with Extended Family (17.4%)

I know many people who have come to terms with their false assumption that extended family wouldn't be a problem in marriage. There's a woman I know who can vouch for the reality check of dealing with extended family. For her, being married to her husband was the easy part, but dealing with his extended family was the hard part. "Being married to his family has been a million times harder than I could have ever imagined. I just wish I would have had some sort of idea of what was coming with the package. It would have made the first five years of marriage so much easier, or maybe I wouldn't have gone through with it from the beginning." Over the years, I've witnessed this couple set boundaries around their marriage to protect it from the potential stress of dealing with extended family. Their marriage continues to thrive, and has grown in love and respect for each other. But that's not to say it hasn't come with hardships.

When you choose a spouse, whether or not you realize it, you ultimately get their whole family as well. If you're single, it's important to be prepared for this reality and learn as much as you possibly can about the family before you become one of them. And for those of us who are married, it's important to continually prioritize our marriages by setting boundaries with our extended family that simultaneously encourage relationship and reduce conflict (more on boundaries in the next chapter).

I know one young man who is currently dealing with the verbal "stings" his mother-in-law tends to throw his way through subtle criticism. But rather than allow that interaction to destroy their marriage, he and his wife have learned to come together, take each other's side, and set boundaries for the type of interactions they choose to engage in with her. Even in these types of situations, we need to learn to "choose marriage" for our relationships to come out better and stronger.

### Personality Differences (16.1%)

It's said that opposites attract. We tend to be drawn to people who possess the qualities, strengths, and personality traits we lack. It's not uncommon for an introvert to be married to an extrovert. Or for the funny guy to be married to the serious gal. Or for the laid-back person to be married to the structured person. And it makes sense, because we are often attracted to people who add something to our life. So yes, opposites do attract. But then as I like to go on and say, "Opposites attract, but then they attack." I know, I know. Leave it to me to be Debbie Downer, right? But seriously, this is the exact scenario I witness constantly in couples counseling, and even in my own marriage. The very same personality traits that draw you to someone initially are the exact traits that can cause conflict and strife later on in your relationship.

John and I have some significant differences in our personalities. I remember specifically during our time of premarital counseling, the counselor turned to us and said, "Deb, you're the gas pedal. John, you're the brakes." He meant I tend to be the personality in the relationship that wants to get things done. My motto in life is "If I don't do it, no one will." I like goals, checklists, agendas, schedules, and plans. I like life to be outlined so I know exactly what needs to get done. One of my best friends jokes with me that I probably even have bullet points for my phone conversations. I tend to go, go, go. That's what the gas pedal does, right?

Whereas John, on the other hand, is definitely the brakes in the relationship. His motto in life would probably be "No worries; it'll get done." He's relaxed, laid back, and more interested in enjoying the present moment than thinking about the next one. I didn't realize exactly how laid back he was until one of our phone conversations while we were dating. He was living in Boston at the time, and I was living in Pennsylvania, so we had a lot of long-distance phone calls that often lasted hours. This particular Sunday afternoon he had to go out to his car to grab something while we were still chatting on the phone.

"Oh, wow," he said calmly, but suddenly.

"What's up?" I replied.

"Hm. Nothing major. I just noticed my car is completely totaled in my driveway." And then without skipping a beat, he went on with the conversation. "Anyway, I'll deal with it a little later. What were you saying?"

"*What!* Your car is *totaled*? Call the police! Figure out what happened! *Go deal with it!*" I urgently suggested.

I couldn't believe how laid back he was about this ordeal. But looking back after a decade of marriage, this isn't an isolated incident in how my husband reacts to stressful situations in life. This is part of who he is. The glimpses I got of his laid-back personality during our time of dating were such an accurate reflection of who my husband is, because what you see in dating, you will always see in marriage. But in marriage, it gets magnified—for better or for worse. For the most part, the differences in this aspect of our personalities have really worked to our benefit. He has taught me so much about slowing down, savoring life, and enjoying each other; whereas I've influenced him to plan ahead, set goals, and really make the most of the time we've been given. We've rubbed off on each other over the years, and we've learned to appreciate each other's perspectives.

But if we're not careful, our personality differences can also cause us to butt heads with trivial things like chores around the house. Sometimes I feel like something needs to get done, and he thinks it can wait. Or more important things, like the time I was experiencing what turned out to be a significant physical health issue. In my urgency to find out what was wrong, his "laid-backness" came across to me as apathy. It hurt me deeply, and made me feel like I wasn't as important to him. After a pretty big argument, we sat down and talked about it. I voiced my hurts, and he clarified his intentions. From his perspective, even though he was deeply concerned, he didn't want to show any signs of panic for fear it would get me worked up even more. He was trying to protect me from feeling fear and anxiety. We were able to see each other's perspectives and get on the same page. But you see how opposites can end up "attacking"? It takes a serious commitment to understand each other by way of communication to allow our personality differences to become an asset rather than a point of contention. Whether we are extroverted or introverted, laid-back or motivated, a thinker or a feeler, a leader or a follower, the many different layers to our personalities need to be both understood and expressed throughout marriage. If you're looking for a fantastic way to assess, understand, and express your specific personality type, pick up a copy of *Please Understand Me II* by David Keirsey. It's an oldie, but a goodie.

*Gender Roles and Family Traditions (making up the last 4%)*

The last two reality checks people reported experiencing in their marriages only made up 4 percent of the population, but I felt it important to add them, particularly in light of Christian tradition and the changing modern family. For some couples, particularly those who come from a more traditional perspective, managing gender roles in marriage can come with some major conflict.

I counseled a couple for whom this became a major issue about two years into their marriage. Having met in high school and married shortly after, they didn't anticipate the tension their different views on family and gender roles would present. He was a hardworking country boy who wanted to provide for his wife and family. She was a talented, driven entrepreneur who wanted to take her business to the next level. But eventually his desire for a traditional family setting (the husband works while the wife stays home and takes care of the kids) clashed with her desire to maximize her talents and grow her business. Frankly, she didn't want to stay home, and he didn't want her to work. They couldn't figure out how to get over the hurdle of their differences in expectations, something they had never really discussed or anticipated going into marriage. After a few short counseling sessions, in which neither of them were willing to pursue a middle ground or sacrifice in any way, they decided to divorce.

> It's less about choosing tradition,
> and more about choosing marriage.

It's heartbreaking when something such as this proves to be the breaking point in a marriage relationship. Sometimes we come with such ingrained beliefs on gender roles and family tradition that we can't differentiate needs from preferences. But this doesn't have to be the case for every marriage. There is always a better way, a middle ground that can be found for those who are willing to choose marriage versus choosing self. I have witnessed many people deciding to put their marriage above their expectations of gender roles and family traditions by saying, "No matter what it takes, we will make this work." Whether it was a wife or husband putting aside a career to stay home with the children, a couple deciding to both pursue their careers and opt for childcare, or a mix of something in between, many couples have together learned the importance of laying aside their presupposed gender roles and ultimately doing whatever is best for their marriage and for their family. I'm happy to say that more and more I am seeing this topic become less and less of an issue in our generation today. It's less about choosing tradition, and more about choosing marriage.

## Embracing Reality

Every single marriage will experience a moment (or many) when the expectations of marriage are met with the reality of marriage, whether it's significant things, like the ones mentioned above, or even smaller things. In each of these moments we are given the opportunity to embrace reality or to continue to live in our fantasy of what we think marriage should be like. One of the reasons I continue to pour into the ministry God has entrusted to me at TrueLoveDates.com is that I firmly believe the more we know, the better we'll do. This applies to every aspect of life, relationships, and marriage. Knowledge equips us with understanding, and understanding sets us up for success. When we know what to expect along the journey of marriage and relationships, we'll be much more likely to choose the right path and make the right choices along the way. Whether you are currently single or married, it's important to prepare yourself for the reality of marriage by understanding that each of the six categories above will come with a set of hardships in some way, shape, or form; and then do your best to learn and prepare for those times.

One thing I love about Jesus is that He was so good at giving us reality checks, preparing us for what life would really be like so we would be empowered to face it when the time came. My favorite reality check in Scripture is found in John 16. Jesus warns His disciples in detail of all the difficult hardships they will ultimately face so they won't be surprised when they happen. The best remedy for dealing with our false expectations is to immerse ourselves in truth. After disclosing these hard things to them, Jesus says,

> I have told you all this so that you won't lose your faith when you face troubles...I have told you all this now to prepare you. So when the time comes for these things to happen, you will remember that I warned you (John 16:1,4 ERV).

But my favorite truth in this entire passage filled with the reality check of the Christian life is that our sweet Jesus ends His teaching with the most powerful truth of all: "I have told you these things so that you can have peace in me. In this world you will have troubles. But be brave! I have defeated the world!" (John 16:33 ERV).

I read His words and my eyes well up with tears—tears in knowing the truth that my Lord loves us so much that He chooses to gently prepare us for the hardships we will face. In this world, we will face troubles. Troubles in our lives, troubles in our relationships, troubles in our jobs, and troubles in our marriages. But above and beyond all these troubles, we serve a God who leaves us with peace in knowing that He is so much greater than any trouble we will ever face. The reality checks of life are met by the reality of a victorious King, who has defeated every difficult thing this world could throw our way. We are to be brave in the fight, knowing and believing that if we persevere, we will ultimately overcome as He has overcome! Can I get an amen?

Even in the reality of the struggles we may face in our relationships and in our marriages, we have the ultimate hope that our God can make a way where there seems to be no way. He can give us everything we need to win our daily battles. No matter what reality check you are facing in your marriage, or will one day face, my prayer for you is that your eyes will close to the false expectations you've created and in turn be opened to the *greater* reality: greater is the God who is in you than the troubles of this world. Be brave and press on, believing that because He has overcome, so can you.

## REFLECTION QUESTIONS
## FOR MARRIED COUPLES

1. What has been the biggest "reality check" for you about marriage? Together, compare some of your false expectations premarriage to the reality of marriage.

2. Which of the top six struggles listed have appeared in your marriage, and in what ways have they caused conflict? What steps have you taken, or what steps do you need to take, to resolve that conflict? Consider this: do any of these aspects possibly require the help of a professional counselor to navigate them?

3. What differences and similarities do you see in your personality types? In what ways can these cause struggles in your marriage? In what ways can these be an asset in your marriage?

# REFLECTION QUESTIONS
# FOR SINGLES

1. In what ways have your family of origin, friendships, or past relationships shaped your assumptions and views of marriage in the following areas: finances, lifestyle differences, extended family, sexual issues, personality differences, and gender roles?

2. Out of over 1000 singles surveyed for this chapter, the majority did not realize married couples so often struggle in the ways highlighted in this chapter (except for finances). Consider meeting with a married couple or married mentor you trust and look up to. Bring a list of questions to ask them about the "reality check" of marriage.

3. What is your personality type and how do you express it to others? Consider reading through *Please Understand Me II* by David Keirsey and learning as much as you can about who you are standing alone. The more you know, the better you'll do!

# Always Use Protection

*From Insecurity to Safety*

M arried couples should always use protection."
The echo of that statement hung in the air as we looked out at the audience, which seemed to be looking back at us with blank stares. John and I were doing our first official talk *together* at a marriage gathering where we had been invited to share, and we wanted to start the talk with a statement the crowd would remember. (Although judging by the looks on their faces, we probably won't use that line at the start of our next talk!) But we weren't talking about "using protection" as in condoms; we were simply sharing our hearts about one of our favorite subjects: protecting marriage.

Speaking of marriage, the first day of ours started with some laughs. So many funny things happened on our wedding day. Allow me to reminisce.

## The Wrong Hand

It's the most serious portion of the wedding ceremony: the exchanging of rings and repeating of our vows. When it's my turn to put the ring on John's finger, he blanks on which hand he's supposed to give me, and puts out both of his hands. I see both of his hands, and my brain blanks as well. My mind starts to race and I start to panic because it's such an important moment, yet I have no idea which hand to put the ring on. *Is it the right hand or the left hand? My right or his right? His left or my left?* I have no clue. Apparently, we weren't paying much attention at rehearsal the night before. But with 300 people staring at us, I quickly choose a hand and hope for the best. No one will even notice anyway, right? *Wrong.* Leave it to my loud and rambunctious family to call me out at my wedding!

"Wrong hand!" someone yells from the back of the crowd.

And then *everyone* starts laughing.

After the laughter died down, I turned to them and said, "Wrong hand, but at least I've got the right guy!" That statement sent everyone into another laughing uproar, and it took us a few minutes to all compose ourselves before we could move forward and get the rings on the *right* hand (well, *left*, but you know what I mean). John still jokes with me today that that moment was, is, and always will be the *highlight* of my comedy career. I always respond by saying, "It was only the beginning, baby."

## The Nursery Blocks

We weren't sure if we were at our wedding or the start of a parenting seminar. We hadn't discussed his message before the start of the wedding, so we looked at each other puzzled when the pastor pulled out a handful of nursery blocks from his front pocket. Everyone in the church started to giggle a bit. But each shape—a triangle, square, and circle—came with a marriage lesson, and as he began speaking it was clear that this funny moment was about to turn into a powerful message.

After ten years of marriage, the lesson that comes back to me most often from those nursery blocks is the lesson of the circle. "The circle," he said, "is a reminder of the importance of drawing a line around your marriage. A barrier of protection; the boundaries that will keep your marriage strong."

## The Circle of Marriage

Anything of value is worth protecting. And marriage is certainly something of value. I can guarantee you with almost 100 percent certainty that if you're reading this book you fall into one of two categories: either you are struggling in your own marriage or you know of someone who is. And adding the word *Christian* in front of the term *marriage* doesn't make you—or anyone else—less susceptible to the struggles you will face and the "intruders" that you'll battle. To protect your marriage, you have to be deliberate about drawing a circle of boundaries around it from the moment it begins, keeping it safe from within and protected from without.

## What Is a Boundary?

Thanks to the groundbreaking work of Drs. Henry Cloud and John Townsend, Christians are talking a lot more about the importance of boundaries.[1] Simply put, a boundary is a limit you set with the purpose of keeping yourself and/or your relationship safe from harm.

I never thought I would be a "white picket fence" kind of person. When I imagined my idea of the perfect home, I can't say it ever included a fence. I'm an extrovert who loves to interact with people and have heart-to-heart conversations with strangers I've only just met, so the thought of having such a clear border around my home totally goes against my personality. But when my husband and I were house shopping a few summers ago, all I wanted was a house with a fence! So what changed over the past decade? One word: children!

Though I am not a "fence" person per se, I love the thought of a fence around my house because it assures me that my children will have limits, and that they'll be kept safe. And while we didn't land on a house with a white picket fence, I love our home because it's surrounded with a "fence" of trees and shrubbery. My kids know exactly how far they can play and wander, based on which trees they're allowed to pass. They've affectionately named the last tree in the back border of our home Tree-ee, and every kid around here knows not to pass Tree-ee. The limits we set are what keep them safe and secure, while still allowing them to have some freedom. Boundaries are an important part of life, of parenting, and of marriage.

All throughout Scripture we find the concept of boundaries being modeled in how God interacts with us, His beloved bride. Because of His deep love for us and in His desire to pursue an intimate relationship with us, He sets limits for us that help our hearts stay aligned with His. Go back with me to the very beginning, to the Garden of Eden. God had just created Adam and provided for him a beautiful garden, the epitome of paradise, as a place to call home:

> GOD planted a garden in Eden, in the east. He put the Man he had just made in it. GOD made all kinds of trees grow from the ground, trees beautiful to look at and good to eat. The Tree-of-Life was in the middle of the garden, also the Tree-of-Knowledge-of-Good-and-Evil (Genesis 2:8-9 MSG).

In His deep love for Adam, the first thing God did after He created Eden was to set some clear boundaries. There was a limit on what Adam *could* and *couldn't* do to maintain the best possible relationship he could have with God. God wanted His relationship with Adam to succeed, and so He reminded him of the boundaries:

> GOD took the Man and set him down in the Garden of Eden to work the ground and keep it in order. God commanded the Man, "You can eat from any tree in the garden, except from the Tree-of-Knowledge-of-Good-and-Evil. Don't eat from it. The moment you eat from that tree, you're dead" (Genesis 2:15-17 MSG).

From the book of Genesis all the way to today, God loves us so much that He's willing to go above and beyond in protecting our relationship with Him, offering us limits that keep us safe and secure. Limits that keep us from wandering too far and getting hurt along the way. Boundaries were a part of that very first interaction modeled between God and man, and every relationship since that time has needed boundaries to survive and thrive to the best of its ability.

Marriage is no different. Every marriage needs boundaries, limits that keep the bad things out and the good things in. You will either set boundaries to keep you close or find yourself wandering farther away than you ever intended. Marriage is our sacred space, but it's up to us to make it that way. In 1 Corinthians 13:7, we read that one attribute of love is protection: "[Love] always protects." Love doesn't simply stay safe on its own; you have to learn to protect it. You must be deliberate, active, and aware to keep it safe. But the word *protection* implies there must be something to protect *from*. To really protect love, you have to be aware of the things that can harm love.

## Why Boundaries?

No one wakes up in the morning and says, "I think I'm going to destroy my marriage today." Major relationship problems usually start with small, innocent steps. Based on the work I do as a professional counselor, I find that most situations involving a marriage issue or affair start with something innocent, like a harmless conversation or a friendly interaction. Zero feelings. Zero ill intentions. It's not the conversation itself that leads to an affair; it's the repetition of conversations, interactions, or behaviors with someone of the opposite sex being used to fill an unmet need or as an escape. I know that sounds extreme to some people, especially if you're not yet married, but hear me out on this. Every person will experience a moment (or even a season) in marriage when they are struggling with unmet needs. And suddenly, that innocent interaction, behavior, or conversation can turn into something just a little bit deeper.

This isn't an uncommon occurrence. In my survey of over 1000 married people of a predominately Christian demographic, 10 percent reported already dealing with infidelity at some point in their marriage. To think that one out of ten married men and women in your circle of friends is likely to face infidelity is heart wrenching. And the national statistics on infidelity in marriage are *much higher*. No one goes into marriage expecting that this kind of tragedy will ever occur. But it's the small mistakes and poor choices that ultimately lead to the larger mistakes. This is why it's important to set limits and establish accountability long before an issue arises.

My husband is an ophthalmologist, which means he operates on eyes to help people restore their sight. Most of the time it's a very rewarding job. But other times, it's heartbreaking. In his line of work, he's witnessed some of the most unfortunate situations where people have lost their vision because of a simple lack of protection. They didn't protect their eyes when they needed to. Whether people are working a construction job, setting off fireworks, or playing a simple game in the backyard, many times unexpected accidents happen. Which is why you'll notice there's a plethora of eye protection around our house—eye goggles and glasses of every shape and size. Like my husband always tells his patients, "No one ever plans to have an accident. You've got to be proactive in protecting your vision when you have the chance." The very same line of thinking applies to relationships: no one ever plans to make a mistake. No one goes into marriage anticipating that something detrimental might someday occur. Putting boundaries in place is the very thing that helps us protect our marriage from what could cause major damage.

Boundaries are most protective before temptation comes up.

The problem is that most people end up putting boundaries into place *after* something problematic happens in their relationship rather than before. They wait until feelings have been hurt, lines have been crossed, and trust has been shattered. But boundaries are most protective before temptation comes up. If you're in a good place right now in your relationship, this is the best time to think through what your boundaries are and how you'll work to achieve those boundaries as a couple. As counterintuitive as this may sound, boundaries give you more freedom in a relationship. They eliminate the need to be controlling in a marriage because the limits set in place are ones you commit to as a couple. They're the expectations and standards you choose to set long before something harmful happens. Boundaries are the circle you choose to draw around your marriage, protecting it *together*.

## The Three Intruders

As a relationship counselor, I naturally find myself working with people who've been through some of the harder things of marriage, namely, infidelity. If you ask someone walking through the painful journey of adultery to identify the biggest intruder in their relationship, they might quickly point the finger at the uninvited third party in the marriage. I had a conversation with a young woman just a few weeks after she found out her husband had cheated on her. Upon learning the news, the *first* thing she did was call the woman her husband cheated with. She picked up the phone and screamed at this unwanted intruder, telling her how she'd destroyed their marriage. And she's not the first person to react this way when faced with such excruciatingly painful news. This reaction is a natural response, because when faced with this type of tragedy, we just want someone to blame. We want to identify the enemy and deal with them as soon as possible. But sometimes the enemy of marriage is a much more subtle intruder.

Over the course of my career working and interacting with

married couples, I've noticed three general areas that tend to become problem spots if boundaries aren't discussed and put into place. I call them the three intruders, and it's safe to say that these intruders tend to sneak in and slowly begin to destroy a marriage long before the "third party" of infidelity comes along.

### Intruder 1: Misplaced Emotions

Long before the start of any inappropriate extramarital relationship comes the seed of misplaced emotions. What I mean by that is emotions and conversations that should be reserved for our spouse begin to be expressed, or incorrectly positioned, toward others. To expand on the situation with the couple I mentioned above, little by little the husband found himself sharing more and more of his emotions with a coworker and less and less with his wife. The conversations he was having outside of his marriage were starting to grow deeper and more significant than the conversations he was having with his spouse. And after the birth of their first child, it was even easier to make excuses for why communication was decreasing at home. They were both tired, drained, and caring for a newborn baby. Before they knew it, level 1, 2, 3, and 4 conversations (that we learned about in chapter 3) were starting to happen more frequently outside of the marriage than inside.

Within months, these conversations not only became more intimate, but lengthier. Soon he found himself spending extra time after work to connect with his coworker, either by calling her on his drive home or grabbing a cup of coffee with her at a nearby coffee shop. And eventually, one small decision at a time, this young married man found himself crossing boundaries that ultimately led him down the path to cheating on his wife, something he vowed he would never do.

Protecting your marriage in the small things is of utter importance, because it's rarely one big, bad decision, but rather a series of small, more subtle decisions that accumulate into something more. Song of Songs identifies the small things as the "little foxes" of a relationship, seemingly insignificant things that can ultimately do some serious damage. "Catch for us the foxes, the little foxes that ruin the vineyards, our vineyards that are in bloom" (Song of Songs 2:15). It's important to guard ourselves from interactions that give someone else a part of us that belongs to our spouse.

If we find we tend to share our feelings and our frustrations with someone other than our spouse, we should take a step back and ask ourselves why. Are we harboring negative feelings? Grievances we haven't shared? Are there communication differences we haven't addressed? Have hurts been swept under the rug? Do priorities need to be reestablished? Whatever it might be, we need to get to the root of the obstacles that might be holding us back from our spouse and do our part in resolving those issues and reestablishing connection with our spouse. For some of you, this may require the help of a professional counselor to help you break through any communication barriers and obstacles you might be facing.

Even when our communication is thriving at home, and our priorities are in the right place, there needs to be great caution when sharing our hearts with someone of the opposite sex. Some parts of us are magnetic when shared with another, and for that reason they should be shared with only our spouse. I choose to partake in certain conversations with *only* my husband, and he only with me.

I have even found there to be truth in this matter when it comes to same-sex relationships. Women in particular love to connect with one another on a deeper level, and there's absolutely nothing wrong with that. Connecting with other women is not only important, but it's a necessary part of establishing community with the people God has placed in our lives. The problem comes when those innocent interactions are *taking the place* of the deep connection we are meant to have with our spouse. A lot of communication between spouses is lost because it is finding its way out through other relationships. Too often, people find themselves sharing with everyone *except* their spouse. Venting to our friends about our marriage can be enough of an out to keep us from venting to our spouse, causing us to avoid our problems rather than resolve them.

I was working with a young woman who was having a hard time grasping this concept. A newlywed, she had only been married for a short time and was in the process of adjusting to the lifestyle of marriage. Before marriage, she had a very close relationship with her sister. They had always talked about everything from the day-to-day things to deep, dark secrets. But now, in marriage, she was finding her default response was to go to her sister even before she went to her husband. Whenever she and her husband experienced any kind of tension in their marriage, she immediately went to her sister to process it instead of learning how to process it with her husband. She brought her sister into their relationship by sharing the intimate details of her marriage, details that she owed to her husband first and foremost.

Not only can venting to others keep us from having these important conversations with our spouse, but consistently speaking negatively about our spouse with others outside the marriage can cause major damage to our spouse's relationship with our family and friends. In every marriage, so many minor problem spots will come up on a regular basis that you'll likely forget about them because of the nature of the marriage relationship. But others won't.

A friend of mine, whom we'll call Sarah, had to learn this the hard way. Early on in her marriage, she told her mom about every bit of tension and conflict she and her husband, whom we'll call James, were experiencing. But as often happens in marriage, Sarah and James would eventually make up and move on, but her mom continued holding on to the negative things Sarah had told her about James. Eventually, James's relationship with Sarah's mom was severed because she couldn't move past her negative view of her son-in-law, even when those issues had already been dealt with and resolved. Unlike Sarah, Sarah's mom knew all the negatives of their marriage, but she didn't get to experience the positives. Venting to friends and family can cause damage to our spouse's relationships with those very people, because while we often move on and experience reconciliation, those negative things we shared are "seared" into their memories indefinitely.

> The goal of a healing conversation should always be reconciliation, not just release.

The key in preventing the intruder of emotional misplacement is simple: your spouse comes first. It's important to be proactive about *always* connecting with your spouse first on the important matters of your life: sharing your heart, your feelings, your struggles, your stressors, your frustrations, and your dreams. We are created to connect, so we will either bring that need to our spouse or allow it to be filled by others.

Now, that's not to say we are never to share anything outside of our marriage. Some hard things in marriage may call for a trusted third party to come in and help us work through a challenging area by offering us wisdom, prayer, and counsel, and speaking into our situation. Sometimes we need to rely on the opinions of trusted friends and family, or the help of a professional counselor to navigate through the difficult areas where we feel stuck in our relationship. But we should always do so for the purpose of inviting healing into our relationship, rather than simply venting. The goal of a healing conversation should always be reconciliation, not just release. One way to discern this is to ask, "Is this person part of the solution?" Meaning, do they have a direct role in helping my spouse and me navigate this issue? If the answer is no, then you're likely inviting the intruder of misplaced emotions.

## Intruder 2: Private Interactions

I heard a heartbreaking, gut-wrenching story about a pastor who confessed to 15 years of infidelity after 25 years of marriage. His wife wrote an article using a pen name and opened up about the details of the secret life her husband had been living right under her nose.[2] What stuck out to me from her story were the private interactions her husband was having with women over the years, under the guise of a prayer meeting or a ministry meeting. I'm not saying private interactions will always lead to infidelity, because that's simply not true. But I am saying private interactions with the opposite sex outside of our spouse's knowledge or awareness sets the stage for boundaries to be crossed. Whether a private meeting, a series of private emails, or an exchange of private texts, if it's an interaction we're deliberately keeping from our spouse, it's a red flag that we've got something to hide.

A megachurch on the West Coast invites me out to speak a few times a year. One thing I love about this church is how proactive they are in protecting their leadership by setting boundaries in place for their staff. In fact, they go above and beyond. One of their specific boundaries has to do with opposite-sex interactions. If you are a married person interacting with someone of the opposite sex, there has to be a *third* party present. Whether an interaction is in the office, at a coffee shop, or in the car to a meeting, they believe proactively avoiding private interactions with the opposite sex is just another small way to protect your marriage. Inviting a third party into the conversation or meeting brings the interaction from private to public.

Some people would consider this legalistic behavior. I know, because I recently published an article about boundaries on my blog and some people were up in arms about it. The article was written by a friend of mine, a pastor's wife, who encouraged married people to avoid intimate friendships with the opposite sex. But something about that boundary really struck a nerve with some of my readers. "Affairs don't happen just by talking to someone of the opposite sex," the comments argued. While this statement is absolutely true, here's the question I pose in reply: What does it hurt to have boundaries in place? What does it hurt to go above and beyond in protecting your marriage from a moment of weakness or a series of mistakes? What does it hurt to set boundaries that would protect your heart and your spouse's heart?

In my years of marriage counseling, I have never once interacted with a couple who said they regret having too many boundaries in their marriage. Literally, not one single time. And I can guarantee you, I'll never, ever, ever hear those words. The only thing I hear, time and time again, is the opposite. "We didn't think about boundaries. We didn't talk about them. We didn't realize we needed them." In fact, 25 percent of the married people I surveyed reported that boundaries and limits are the one thing they discuss the least in their marriage. It's time to start changing the conversation, creating an atmosphere of openness and honesty in our marriage relationships where we've got nothing to hide. Boundaries help us to create a relationship that's so transparent and authentic that even the thought of hiding a private interaction has no fertile soil in which to grow.

Some of you have likely had some of these hard discussions with your spouses and apply some type of boundaries to your marriage. But for many of you, namely that 25 percent who never talk about boundaries, I know this is foreign territory. I recently heard from a woman who was days away from getting married, and she shared that she and her fiancé had never even thought through this concept, much less applied any type of boundaries to their relationship. "We don't need boundaries," she said. "We just trust each other." Let me go on record loud and clear. Healthy boundaries are not about a lack of trust. Healthy boundaries are about protection. And like I said before, anything of value is worth protecting.

So, practically, what does it look like in a marriage to set limits around private conversations? I tread cautiously with this subject because I don't think there's a cookie-cutter approach to setting boundaries that can be applied to all married couples. There's no set of rules or one-size-fits-all approach because different couples have different personalities, comfort levels, and past experiences. But the underlying theme is transparency, and always choosing marriage.

For the sake of offering examples, I'll share some boundaries John and I found to work well for us. For one, we try to be as inclusive as we can with each other when it comes to one-on-one interactions with the opposite sex. If one of us is invited to a get-together with someone of the opposite sex, we make it a priority to go together and avoid meeting alone with that person. Now, obviously, because of the nature of our jobs, working with clients and patients requires us to have a professional level of one-on-one interactions. But when it comes to our personal lives, we loop in each other and include each other in all our face-to-face interactions with friends, acquaintances, and coworkers of the opposite sex. John and I are a team, and we make sure our social lives always reflect that to others as well.

Another thing we do to include each other is to be transparent with our digital interactions. In these days of texting, emails, and social media, a person can easily become engaged in a life of private interactions without even being aware they were going down that path. So for us, when it comes to emailing and texting friends and acquaintances of the opposite sex, we go out of our way to include each other by either telling the other about the conversation or simply copying our spouse into the interaction. Not only does it serve to keep us transparent, but it gives us a deeper connection with each other because our social lives are interwoven as well. It's just one more thread that ties us together and gives us more common ground. For us, it's a win-win, and it's kept our marriage strong and consistently taken our trust to deeper and deeper levels.

Like I said before, there's no list of rules I can give you for your own marriage, because boundaries neither can nor should be forced on a spouse. You build them together. I challenge you to set some time aside to work together to build the fences in your life that will keep the good things in and the dangerous things out.

### Intruder 3: Wasted Time

Did you know a third of all divorce filings in 2011 included the word *Facebook*? I was completely stunned when I stumbled upon that statistic in an article from the *Washington Times*.[3] But logically, looking at the way our society functions and the massive influence social media has on our interactions, it really shouldn't be surprising at all. Think of how much time and energy are being poured into not only social media, but our digital devices in general. Time that we could be spending connecting with one another in intimate and meaningful ways is being replaced by the superficial, yet extremely addicting adrenaline rush of our online connections. In a recent study, researchers found a strong positive correlation between the number of Facebook accounts in each state and the number of divorces that occurred in that same state. Even when other contributing factors were controlled, such as economic and socio-demographic factors, the results still held up! While all these things don't imply that Facebook *causes* divorce or marital distress, they certainly reflect a new set of challenges this generation of marriages is dealing with. This is something our parents' generation didn't even have to think about. This is why so many people, me included, resonated with the words of my friend and fellow author, Jarrid Wilson, when he wrote a blog post stating he was "Getting a Divorce."

> Before you start assuming I will be leaving my wife, let me just tell you that's just simply not the case. I'm looking to leave someone else. Someone you may not know about. Someone who takes up most of my time, distracts me from spending time with my wife, and even spends time with me during the late hours of the night.
>
> Her name is iPhone...She's extremely smart, funny, reliable, and keeps me up to date with all the latest trends. And although she's always by my side, I can't help but notice that she is keeping me from spending time with

the people who matter most in my life: God, my wife, my family, and my dreams.

She's really good at keeping my attention. So much so that I've been known to completely ignore people when they are trying to have a conversation with me. She tempts me to use her apps while at church, weddings and funerals, instead of enjoying the moment un-distracted. She even keeps me from working on personal projects that have strict deadlines.

She's extremely insensitive when it comes to my safety, and is always tempting me to be with her while I drive. I can't help but notice she is slowly infecting my social life, my marriage, and the lives of those around me. Many people act like it's no big deal, but I imagine the longer one ignores this issue, the worse one's personal relationships will be affected in the long run.[4]

I loved this article, because there's so much truth here. So much of our time and energy is voluntarily given away to this sly and subtle intruder. There's no denying the negative impact social media has had on our lives, and specifically on our marriages. Not only do we lose a significant amount of our time, but because of the psychological nature of social media, we also lose our inhibition. Behind the screen of a device, many people find themselves engaging in activities, conversations, or behaviors they would not have otherwise even considered doing. An article released by Focus on the Family tells the sad story of a woman who forfeited her 16-year marriage over an emotional affair that began with a private message in her inbox from a guy she casually dated in high school. The married mother of three began privately communicating with this gentleman. The casual messaging eventually turned into hour-long conversations, in which a deep emotional connection and romantic attraction developed. Her marriage eventually came to an end, triggered by a series of social media interactions with a man from her past with whom she never even reunited face-to-face. And this story is not an isolated incident. I've heard countless stories of men and women who lost their marriages and families because of someone they met or interacted with online. It's a sad phenomenon that we didn't have to deal with 20 years ago, but one we can't continue to ignore.

> It's important for us to prioritize where we allow our time to go or we'll find that we've quickly exchanged the intimate for the inanimate.

It doesn't have to take an affair for us to realize how quickly our time and energy are slipping away. How often do we also find that, through the lure of social media, we're spending more time casually learning about acquaintances and even strangers than we are learning about the people who are most significant in our lives? Wasted time is the quietest of intruders, but one that is ravaging many homes because of its silent entrance. Our time is literally our most valuable commodity, and it should be invested in the people we love and cherish the most. And not just the *quantity* of time, but the *quality* of our time. Nowadays, two people can be in the same room and not spend time with each other at all. If we're not careful to set boundaries around our time, we'll find it slowly slipping away. It's important for us to prioritize where we allow our time to go or we'll find that we've quickly exchanged the intimate for the inanimate.

Protecting our marriage from the intruder of wasted time means we set limits on where and how we will spend our time, and who we will spend our time with. It sounds like a no-brainer that it's important to invest our time into our marriage, doesn't it? But the reality of what is actually happening in marriages today is alarming. In a survey, I asked singles to answer how they perceived married couples spend their time. The majority assumed that married couples spend most of their free time together. But in my survey of married people, 54 percent reported they *do not* spend their free time together, but rather invest in their separate hobbies and interests. Think about all the time being poured into things outside of the marriage relationship, both passively (through social media) and directly (through separate hobbies and interests).

I'm not saying a married couple needs to spend every waking moment together. There's a time and place for separate hobbies, needed free time, and opportunities to invest in friendships with others. I'm all for having a girls' night out every once in a while, or for my husband going out with a buddy to grab some wings and have good conversation. I love being able to carve out some free time to write, or to give my husband some time to work on a house project he's been wanting to do. But the problem I see occurring is that those very same people who are constantly investing in life outside of marriage are doing so at the expense of life inside of their marriage. They're watering their personal lives while their marriages are slowly dying of thirst. They're choosing self instead of choosing marriage.

## Draw Your Circle

In the process of setting boundaries to protect our marriages from the intruders of emotional displacement, private interactions, and wasted time, we've got to be able to take a good hard look at what needs to be changed, and then follow through by taking the steps we need to make that change possible. It's not enough to just want things to get better until we start moving in the direction of better. Maybe that means putting down our phones and devices in exchange for eye contact with our spouse. Maybe it means logging off social media and choosing a meaningful conversation instead. Maybe it means enriching our communication and emotional expression toward our spouse. Maybe it means applying greater caution in our interactions with the opposite sex. Whatever it means, we need to take the time to draw a circle of protection around our marriage by acknowledging the areas in our lives that need boundaries, and then determining to make those boundaries a reality. Everything of value is worth protecting, and the gift of marriage is one of the most valuable things you'll ever be given. So in our actions, behaviors, and interactions— let's choose marriage.

## REFLECTION QUESTIONS FOR MARRIED COUPLES

1. In my survey, 25 percent of married people reported that they rarely discuss boundaries with their spouse. Are boundaries a topic of discussion in your marriage? Why or why not?

2. Regarding the three intruders of marriage, which intruder tends to be the biggest issue in your relationship? In what ways do these three intruders affect your marriage?

   a. Misplaced Emotion

   b. Private Interactions

   c. Wasted Time

3. Together as a couple, take some time to discuss the specific boundaries you have in place regarding each of the three intruders. Do you need to set any additional boundaries in place? Talk this through and then write out your boundaries together.

# REFLECTION QUESTIONS
# FOR SINGLES

1. When it comes to your personal boundaries and interactions with others, do you feel challenged to set specific boundaries for yourself in any aspects of your life (habits, time management, money management, social media, emotional interactions, physical interactions)?

2. One of my favorite quotes is a reminder that "you teach people how to treat you." In what ways are you setting boundaries around your life to protect yourself from harmful interactions with acquaintances, friends, and in dating relationships?

3. As you look at your family of origin or the people closest to you, how have boundaries (or a lack of boundaries) been modeled in the marriages you've witnessed? How did this impact their relationships?

# 7

# #RealTalk

*From Facade to Authenticity*

One of the saddest stories I've ever heard was about a beautiful young woman who leapt to her death from the ninth floor of a parking garage. But the most shocking part of the story is this: no one saw it coming. Looking at her social media account, no one would have guessed this 19-year-old University of Pennsylvania track star was dealing with her own demons. Her "perfect-posted" life would have never tipped you off. Just one hour before she killed herself, she posted a beautiful picture on Instagram of twinkling lights in the city, with the backdrop of a beautiful sunset coming in from behind. What no one knew then is that the sun was about to set on her own young life.[1]

This horrific story really hit home because it reminded me of the secret battles everyone is facing, whether or not we see them. I especially remember a time when I faced a battle, about two months after delivering my second child. I was going through the thick of postpartum depression, and my days were filled with tears, anxiety, and feelings of being overwhelmed with life and all that it entailed. Life felt so dark, and I felt so alone, suffocating beneath it.

But looking at my social media profiles during that time, *you wouldn't have had a clue.* I had just posted a series of photos of my daughter and me making silly faces in the camera. To the rest of the world (and even to her precious little awareness) my life was great. But inside my world felt like it was crumbling. It took everything in me just to get through the regular routine of the day. I remember scrolling through social media that same evening with tears streaming down my face, feeling a wave of depression come over me as it often did. *Why was everyone happy but me? What was wrong with me? Why couldn't I get it together?*

My sweet husband, whose pep talks I could never live without, gently held me and reminded me of the photos I had posted of my daughter and me. I don't remember his exact words, but he said something that has since stuck with me: "Everyone is going through something, but no one posts pictures of their tears."

## Picture Perfect

We live in a world where everyone is out to present their "picture perfect" self through the rose-colored lens of social media. Take a scroll through our Facebook walls and what do we find? Our Pinterest-perfect lives, our elegant meals, and our happiest moments. We are out to show the world the best in us, even when it's not always 100 percent reality. Don't get me wrong. I'm not saying there is anything wrong in putting our best face forward and capturing our highlight reel through social media. But I am saying comparison is the greatest enemy of joy. And even more devastating than comparing our real life to others' real lives is when we compare our "worst" to their "best," as often happens because of the nature of social media.

Pastor Steven Furtick says it like this: "The reason we struggle with insecurity is because we compare our behind-the-scenes with everyone else's highlight reel." I'm afraid we've become so accustomed to showing our highlight reel to the world around us that we've lost the ability to open up about what's going on behind the scenes. It's one thing to know about our brokenness, but it's a whole other thing to learn to share our brokenness with the people we love and trust the most.

> Marriage is an invitation
> to share our brokenness.

Marriage is an invitation to share in that brokenness. It's an opportunity to shed our facade and get real with who we are and what we're struggling with. It's a chance to share our burden with the built-in helper God has given us. God knew we needed this chance when He proclaimed that it is not good for man to be alone (Genesis 2:18). Marriage is our time to declare that, though we will struggle, we will no longer struggle alone.

### To Love, Honor, and Confess

It's incredible to me how very little we talk about the role of confession in relationships within contemporary evangelical Christianity. I can say with confidence that in my lifetime I've heard less than a handful of sermons on the importance of confession within the body of Christ, much less within the context of a marriage. In my survey of over 1000 married people, nearly 50 percent of them reported that confession of their sins and struggles is what they discuss the *least* in their marriage. It's an important discipline that's been lost in our modern-day church and culture at large. But more concerning to me is that it's a discipline that's been lost in our marriages as well.

As a professional counselor, I believe without a shadow of a doubt that confession is an important part of building trust and achieving authenticity and freedom in a marriage relationship. To be known—fully and completely—is one of the greatest feelings two people can experience within the context of a marriage. To be known fiercely and still loved fiercely is an intoxicating kind of love because it's not a love based on who someone thinks you are; it's a love based on who you really are when the facade has been dropped. In his book *The Meaning of Marriage*, Tim Keller says this: "To be loved but not known is comforting but superficial. To be known and not loved is our greatest fear. But to be fully known and truly loved is, well, a lot like being loved by God. It is what we need more than anything. It liberates us from pretense, humbles us out of our self-righteousness, and fortifies us for any difficulty life can throw at us."[2] *To be fully known and truly loved is a lot like being loved by God.* A deep and incomparable love awaits those who are willing to live in transparency and authenticity.

But if that's the case, why is it so hard to let down our facade? Why do we hold on to the masks for so long? Why are so many married people struggling to show their true self to their spouse? One of the reasons I believe confession has been downplayed is this, simply put: it's a very hard thing to do. If apology is asking for forgiveness when you've wronged someone, confession takes it a step further by bringing to light what is in the dark. It means exposing your sins, weaknesses, struggles, and secrets long before they have had a chance to make their way into your relationships. Long before they have had a chance to destroy your life from the inside out.

## The Destruction of Darkness

Many years ago a story broke about a famous 29-year-old married pastor who, after many years in the spotlight of ministry, shocked everyone in his family and congregation by suddenly confessing his secret addiction to pornography. But as I watched this entire story unfold, the surprising part for me was not the addiction. I've worked with countless couples facing the strongholds of sexual addiction at different levels of severity. No, the surprising part of this story was not the addiction, but the lengths to which he'd gone to hide his struggle, and the incredibly painful toll it had taken on his body.

For many years prior, he was so deep into his secret struggle that he couldn't bring himself to tell the people who knew him and loved him the most. But eventually his secret sin and double life began to take a terrible toll on not just his emotional and spiritual health, but his physical health as well. He began to suffer unexplainable health problems, such as frequent vomiting and losing his hair. His secret life was destroying him from the inside out. So he took the lie even further. Instead of telling his loved ones he was struggling with an ongoing pornography addiction, he told them the plethora of health problems stemmed from a terminal illness. For two whole years he fooled his wife, his family, and his entire church into believing he was dying of cancer.

And if this wasn't bad enough, the story just gets worse and worse as his web of lies eventually took over his life. He had to go to great lengths to cover up his secrets, going as far as writing false emails and faking doctor appointments under the guise of a cancer diagnosis that didn't even exist. And in his deep struggle, he wrote and passionately performed a runaway worship song (wearing an oxygen tank while singing) about his need for healing that ended up topping the charts. I think we can all agree that he was certainly in need of healing, just not healing from cancer.

"I've been living a lie for a long time," he said tearfully in an exclusive media interview released shortly after his confession. "I've been hiding who I am for so long...the last two years have been hell physically and emotionally. But I never sat down and said, 'Let's try to fool the world.' It's not as if you sit there and plan the next move...I know I've caused so many people so much pain, but I'm done. I can't keep living like this."[3] After years of living a double life, he confessed his severe addiction to pornography and the consuming grip it had on his life. He explained that growing up surrounded by the Christian culture and the negative stigma this particular sin carried, he felt such a great level of shame that he hadn't been able to get himself to take down his facade and confess. He lived in darkness for so long that he almost lost sight of the light.

## The Darkness Within

It's easy to look at this man's story and think we are so much better off than he is. But before we start casting stones of judgment, I want to take this opportunity to challenge each of us to look at the darkness within our own lives. What are the secret sins, struggles, and battles we're currently facing? What are the unknown battles we fight for in our own spirits and souls daily? What are our signature sins, the sins we could write our names on, because we struggle with them so often? For us to face the darkness within, we must start by calling it out and acknowledging it. We must recognize that it exists. We must start by giving it a name, and bringing it into the light.

Our secret sins and struggles can come in so many different forms. Maybe they don't appear in the blatant form of addiction to pornography, but maybe they come more subtly, in the form of addiction to criticism or judgment. Maybe they sneak into our lives in the form of an overconsumption of alcohol, too much spending, or a life filled with gossip that lives to tear others down. Whatever our secret sins and struggles, we must learn to bring them out of the darkness and into the light, for it is only in the light that sins and struggles begin to lose their stronghold.

## The Light of Life

The Bible often uses the metaphor that sin happens in the darkness and healing happens in the light. Jesus even referred to Himself as the Light. Something very powerful occurs when we allow our lives to be taken from the darkness and brought into the Light. Psychology and Scripture agree that to move into the light of healing we must first bring our sins and struggles out of the darkness. Psychology uses the term *admit* while Scripture often uses the term *expose*, but in either case, the main idea is that we must recognize and reveal the darkness to replace it with the light.

- I have come into the world as a light, so that no one who believes in me should stay in darkness (John 12:46).

- Light has come into the world, but people loved darkness instead of light because their deeds were evil. Everyone who does evil hates the light, and will not come into the light for fear that their deeds will be exposed (John 3:19-20).

- Have nothing to do with the fruitless deeds of darkness, but rather expose them. For it is shameful even to mention what the disobedient do in secret. But everything exposed by the light becomes visible—and everything that is illuminated becomes a light (Ephesians 5:11-13).

- Because of the tender mercy of our God, by which the rising sun will come to us from heaven to shine on those living in darkness and in the shadow of death, to guide our feet into the path of peace (Luke 1:78-79).

- This is the message we have heard from him and declare to you: God is light; in him there is no darkness at all. If we claim to have fellowship with him and yet walk in the darkness, we lie and do not live out the truth (1 John 1:5-6).

The one and only way we move our souls from darkness into light is by confessing our sins and struggles to Jesus. "If we confess our sins, he is faithful and just and will forgive us our sins and purify us from all unrighteousness" (1 John 1:9). Over and over in Scripture we learn that confession plays a significant part in the Christian life, because in confession we are acknowledging our great need for a Savior. *Confessing our sins to our Lord is the only thing that can move us from darkness into light, but confessing our sins to others is what keeps us there.* According to Scripture, confessing our sins to one another is how the process of healing takes place: "Confess your sins to one another and pray for one another, that you may be healed. The prayer of a righteous person has great power as it is working" (James 5:16 ESV). There's no denying that there is power in prayer and confession between two people. How, then, can we apply this important discipline into the framework of our marriages?

## The Five Secrets You Should Never Keep in Marriage

For some of us, confessing our sins to God sounds much easier than confessing to our spouse. I worked with a couple who had never practiced the act of confession. Their marriage was filled with secrets. From little "white lies" to more significant secrets, they didn't feel the freedom to be completely honest and open with each other, and they lived their lives trying to hide the truth. Eventually their web of secrets caught up to them, and they found their marriage in a dark place, barely surviving and struggling to separate the truth from the lies.

As Christians, none of us would argue that the healthiest of marriages are those filled with honesty, authenticity, and transparency. When it comes to the important aspects of life, we could certainly all agree that there is no room in marriage for lies and deceit. But many times the greatest enemy of honesty is not necessarily "dishonesty," as with the couple mentioned above, but rather "omission" by way of a lack of communication. When it comes to day-to-day life in marriage, many people struggle to find the words, or more common yet, to find the time to commit to good communication and confession. But for us to take down the facade and make room for authenticity, certain topics must always make their way "into the light" of marriage. It's only in the light that sins and struggles begin losing their grip over our lives, moving us closer and closer to freedom. When I work with married couples, in both the premarital and marriage counseling setting, I often walk them through five important topics that should never be kept secret from your spouse. These five topics offer some practical guidelines to follow as we move from *facade to authenticity*, one step at a time.

## #1 Past Secrets

If you've been married for quite some time, yet find yourself still holding on to secrets from your past, I recommend you start here. I urge the couples I work with in premarital counseling to work through the skeletons in their closet long before they say "I do." Sexual history, drug/alcohol history, abuse history, and family history are the kinds of things you need to come to terms with in your own life and then share them with your partner. But now the question is posed, How much is too much when it comes to sharing about your past? Is there a level of sharing that can be damaging to a marriage?

There are no quick and easy answers to this question because different couples find themselves in different situations and needing different levels of sharing. Personally, I don't believe it's necessary nor beneficial to discuss every single nitty-gritty detail of your past, but it's important to be able to communicate the general ideas. If you think of your past as one chapter in the book of your life, it's important to honestly summarize that chapter for your spouse, but unnecessary to walk them through every single sentence on every single page.

One incredible couple comes to mind. The man had both a sexual history and a drug abuse history. He hadn't been a Christian in his young adult years, and so his past looked starkly different from his fiancée's. He made a deliberate choice to give her an authentic look into his past. He sat with her and unpacked his drug history, told her he had previous sexual partners, and confessed that pornography had been a general part of his life. He spent some time helping her to understand the negative family environment he came from, because it was so drastically different from hers. For this couple, it wasn't necessary nor beneficial for him to go through the nitty-gritty details about his sexual partners, what their names were, or what his sexual experiences were like. He had a lot of regrets from that time in his life, but it was important for him to share his history with his fiancée, because for him, *although his past is no longer who he is*, it did have an impact on him.

Your *past* doesn't define you, but it certainly shapes you, and you owe it to your partner to give them a glimpse of the things that have made you who you are today—the good, the bad, and the ugly.

## #2 Secret Sins

> It is in the secret that struggles become strongholds.

Whether you have a habitual or once-in-a while problem with sexual struggles or you struggle with emotional eating or compulsive gambling, the worst thing you can do for your marriage is keep your sins and struggles a secret. The devil is a liar, and he longs for you to stay quiet about your struggles with things like masturbation, adultery, pornography, addictions, habitual sinful thoughts, and signature sins. He knows it is in the silence that you will continue to struggle. "No one needs to know," he whispers. "You'll eventually get this under control. You'll only hurt them more by telling them the truth," he lies. But it is in the secret that struggles become strongholds.

I know people who struggled with secret sin for years upon years under the hopes that they could eventually get it under control on their own. I counseled the sweetest-looking little old lady who had been stealing from her company for 25 years, unbeknownst to her friends, family, children, and grandchildren, until she finally got caught after more than $100,000 had gone unaccounted for. That goes to show you that secret sin has no prejudice and can affect anyone and everyone. But healing can happen when we bring our struggles into the light. If you're married and find yourself struggling with a secret sin, talk to your spouse, and then tell a trusted mentor or a seasoned friend. They can all work to support and love you through the nitty-gritty that comes with healing and freedom. If your secret sin is starting to become a regular part of your life, affecting your career, family, or relationships, it's important to immediately seek the help of a professional counselor who can help you assess the severity and differentiate a struggle from an addiction.

### #3 Financial Secrets

Do you have a habit of spending and then hiding? Hiding receipts, bills, or even hiding purchases from your spouse? When it comes to finances in marriage, everything should always be out on the table. Financial dishonesty is one of the most common "secrets" in marriage and causes stress that has been linked to a higher level of dissatisfaction in marriage as well as divorce.[4] The bottom line is that marriage isn't about *my* finances or *your* finances; it's about *our* finances. Learning to become "one" in all things means there is no room for financial secrets. If finances have led to frequent arguments and conflict or secrets in your relationship, it's time to take inventory of your spending habits as a couple. Invite a professional counselor as well as a financial adviser into your situation so you can take back control and create an atmosphere of complete transparency in your marriage.

### #4 Health-Related Secrets

I've interacted with married couples who tend to keep their health issues to themselves. Usually, it comes from a place of good intention, in that they are trying to save their spouse from the stress of worrying about their health. I know of a gentleman who even kept his terminal illness from his wife, in fear of the negative impact it would have on her. But in that deceit, he robbed her of savoring and cherishing her final days with him by her side. The beauty of marriage is that it gives us the opportunity to love and support each other through times of sickness as well as in times of health. As difficult as it is to walk through a major illness or health-related problems (whether physical health or mental health), those times of difficulty offer an opportunity for intimate connection, companionship, and support from one spouse to the other. Be honest and upfront about your medical issues and concerns, and allow your spouse the opportunity to walk by your side.

### #5 Relationship Secrets

Even couples who have no problem being honest in the above categories can sometimes struggle to share their true hearts and feelings about their marriage relationship. When it comes to your marriage, what are your relational needs, and are they being met? Can you open up about your sexual desires, your emotional needs, and your goals and dreams? Can you share your opinions and ideas without the fear of feeling rejected or criticized? Can you talk about what you want, and on the flip side, listen to what your partner is longing for you to work on in the relationship? Out of fear, many couples find themselves holding on to their relational needs rather than sharing those important things with their spouse.

But maybe your relationship secrets are outside of your marriage. Maybe you find yourself feeling a growing attraction toward someone of the opposite sex. Your interactions with that friend at work are becoming increasingly intimate. You're spending more and more time texting with that old boyfriend from high school. You find yourself fantasizing about someone who's not your wife. Maybe it's so subtle you've convinced yourself it's not even worth mentioning. But whatever relationship secrets you find yourself holding on to, hope for healing in all the above areas comes when we learn to recognize our struggle, and then confess it.

## Where Do We Begin?

After reading one of my articles about secrets in marriage, I got a panicked but genuinely concerned email from a gentleman that went like this: "How can any married couple be transparent with each other? That seems completely impossible. In my case, any attempt at the deep kinds of openness you describe would have disastrous consequences. I just can't picture such transparency in any way, shape, or form—it doesn't compute. How can a longtime married couple who just can't reveal themselves to each other with any kind of transparency start doing so, even a little? Can you help me understand what this looks and feels like?"

I know this gentleman is not alone in his fears. For some, the thought of learning to open up after years and years of marriage, or even after growing up in a family that never modeled openness, can seem like an impossible task. In this man's situation, the thought of opening up to his wife about the secret sins and struggles he carried seemed like it would do nothing but destroy their marriage. *Isn't ignorance bliss? Wouldn't it be better for her to live without knowing? What if confession might potentially bring pain and sorrow? Is it even possible to have this kind of honesty in a marriage?*

First, I want to address these questions by starting with the affirmation that it is absolutely possible to have an open and honest environment between a husband and wife. Not only have I experienced this in my own personal life, but I've seen it in the lives of countless other couples as well. It's something we should all continually strive for. But with that in mind, I want to add to that statement something very important: there is a significant difference between speaking the truth and speaking the truth *in love*, which is what the Bible calls us to do (Ephesians 4:15).

Speaking the truth *without* love can be devastating in a marriage and can create a huge barrier between two people. This isn't about being brutally honest; it's about being authentic in a loving way. Love is always the motivator. For some of you, this means simply being brave and starting the hard conversations, in the name of love. Set aside a specific time this coming week to sit down and begin talking through the five areas mentioned above. Practice vulnerability, openness, and honesty by sharing both your victories as well as your struggles, and learning to speak the truth in love.

> Struggle becomes a stronghold when we are living a life marked more by our facade than by our authenticity.

But second, I want to explain that there is a difference between you who are striving to live authentically and you who are living a secret life. The first lives a majority of their life to protect authenticity, whereas the second lives a majority of their life to protect their secrets. We all struggle to be completely authentic, but struggle becomes a stronghold when we are living a life marked more by our facade than by our authenticity. For this man in the email, that was exactly the case. After unpacking his situation some more, it was clear that he was essentially living a double life. There were so many things about his life and secret struggles that his wife was completely unaware of. To sit her down and drop bombs of truth after bombs of truth could have been devastating to their marriage, because it would take her knowledge from 0 to 100.

In cases like this, I believe it's important to call on the help of a professional counselor to help guide you through the process of authenticity. These kinds of secret lives don't just magically happen. They are built brick by brick because of a pattern—things like emotional disconnect, bad habits, spiritual apathy, unhealthy interactions, and a lack of communication—and must be taken down brick by brick as well. If you find yourself in this kind of situation, I urge you to seek the help of a Christian licensed professional counselor and get the process of healing started today.

# #RealTalk

I knew this would be the hardest chapter to write. Before I even had one word written, thinking through this chapter brought a little pit to my stomach. *Well, at least it's toward the end of the book,* I told myself. *I still have time.* But here I am, seven chapters in, finishing the chapter about transparency and authenticity. And my prediction was right. It was a hard chapter to write. Because you know what authenticity means, right? It means we take down our facade. It means we let go of the mask of who we want to be, or who we think we are, or who we want others to believe we are, and come to terms with who we *truly* are. That's not always an easy thing to do, is it? It's not easy for you, or for me, or for anyone. But for those of us who take on this great challenge, there awaits a great freedom. I've seen it, and I've experienced it time and time again in my marriage, in my personal life, in my professional life, and in the lives of the thousands of people I've interacted with and counseled over the years.

So let's just dive in.

Let's take off our masks.

Let's come to terms with our secrets and learn to master the art of being *real* with ourselves, with our God, and with the people He has called us to be real with. Marriage invites us to take down our facade and live authentically. Because only in the Light can we really be set free.

## REFLECTION QUESTIONS
## FOR MARRIED COUPLES

1. Of the five secrets mentioned, are there any you need to discuss with your spouse? If so, set aside a time this week to begin the process of transparency.

2. Take some time to identify your "signature sin"—the sin you struggle with most often. Have you applied the practice of confession to this area of your life? If not, how can you begin to open up to your spouse about it? What is holding you back?

3. When it comes to speaking the truth in love, do you tend to lean toward offering truth without love or love without truth? How can you take steps toward finding that proper balance?

## REFLECTION QUESTIONS
## FOR SINGLES

1. When it comes to living a transparent life, do you have a trusted friend or mentor who can hold you accountable for areas of struggle and sin in your life? If yes, write down the names of two people who come to mind. If no, write down the names of two people you trust and can approach for accountability.

2. Take some time to identify your "signature sin"—the sin you struggle with most often. Have you applied the practice of confession to this area of your life? If not, how

can you begin to open up about it? What is holding you back?

3. When it comes to speaking the truth in love, do you tend to lean toward offering truth without love or love without truth? How can you take steps toward finding that proper balance?

# Sex Marks the Spot

*From Infatuation to Adoration*

They'd been anticipating their wedding night for months. Nothing is going to be better than honeymoon sex, they thought. Enraptured in each other's love, they couldn't wait to finally get to their honeymoon suite and let the evening commence. But as soon as they stepped into the room, it hit them like a ton of bricks: they were completely exhausted from hours of dancing and celebrating with friends and family. Looking around the gorgeous suite, they found rose petals spread all over the bed and candles lit to set the mood. Add to that, some of their friends had broken into their honeymoon suite hours before and left a plethora of condoms, lubricants, streamers, and balloons everywhere to greet the happy (and sexually inexperienced) couple upon their arrival. Exhaustion can wait when you're ready for love.

The couple quickly undressed—and by quickly, I mean they took about half an hour just trying to figure out how to unbutton the 100 tiny white buttons going down the back of the bride's dress. Why doesn't anyone think about how hard these dresses are going to be to take off *after* the wedding? It takes about ten people to help the bride get her dress on before the wedding, and after the wedding she's left with one person—specifically, a groom who knows absolutely nothing about dresses! Okay, I'll get off my soapbox and get back to this funny story.

She finally got out of her dress and slipped into her nightie and by the time they started relaxing it was already almost midnight. And what do you think came next? Well, the realization that they hadn't eaten in over 12 hours, of course! They were starving! Who has time to eat during the excitement and rush of their wedding day? No one. So they opened their mini-fridge, and to their amazement, the hotel crew had packed up the leftovers of their untouched wedding plates, fully equipped with lobster tail, filet mignon, red-velvet cake, and chocolate-covered strawberries. So they did what every married couple does on their honeymoon, right? They stuffed their faces. They spent the next hour delightfully scarfing down leftovers well past midnight and laughing about how *this* was how their honeymoon night was actually going down.

Once their bellies were full, it was finally time for honeymoon sex. But where do you begin when you're both virgins and have absolutely no experience in having sex? Well, you do what your body naturally tells you to do and then see what happens. When it was time for the "big moment," they decided to try some of that lubricant their friends had left them. They'd heard stories of the discomfort that could occur during first-time sex, and lubricant would probably help, they thought. So they looked around the dimly lit room until they found it and quickly lathered some on. To their surprise, it wasn't regular lubricant; it was an intense heating kind, and within minutes they both started feeling the most unexpected and uncomfortable burning sensation that caused them to leap out of bed, looking for something to *wipe this stuff off*! Needless to say, intercourse didn't happen that night. Their first sexual experience was clumsy, it was hilarious, and it was absolutely awkward, but they were in love, and they were together, and that was all that really mattered at the end of the day.

This story always makes me laugh out loud, because it's a glimpse into a real-life honeymoon story—*our* real-life honeymoon story, to be exact. It was one of the funniest evenings, mostly because the expectations we had were so far from the reality of what actually played out. We imagined a lot of wonderful things would happen on that glorious night, and running around the room naked and in total discomfort was definitely not how we expected it to go down. That we would go to sleep *still* virgins on our honeymoon night was so far off our radar. At least we got some incredible leftovers out of it. We laugh about it to this day, and we've never tried heating lubricant again.

Before marriage, we tend to have a romanticized idea of what sex will be like on our wedding night. We imagine an evening of passion and romance, intoxicated by the glorious emotions of the day. We imagine making love to our spouse, with the untamable fire of love burning inside our hearts. We imagine falling asleep in each other's arms, clinging together desperately in love like we often see couples do in the movies. I recently asked singles to describe to me what they thought sex would be like on their honeymoon. One single woman described it in a few blissful words, saying that honeymoon sex would be "tender, thoughtful...a meaningful celebration of the commitment of becoming one." It makes sense that we have such elevated expectations, doesn't it? Honeymoon sex is put on a very high pedestal among Christian men and women because it's what so many of them have been desperately waiting for their entire lives.

## Just Because You Wait Doesn't Make It Great

I think one of the biggest misconceptions about sex is that people assume just because they wait to have it until marriage, their sex life will be magical—guaranteed. We're taught that virginity is the key to a fulfilling sex life come the wedding night. So we start believing that if we save ourselves for marriage, our wedding night will be filled with hours and hours of amazing, hot sex. We imagine all the stars align-ing in that perfect moment, our bodies naturally taking over, know-ing exactly what to do. But when the moment comes, it's never how we thought it would be. I hear from many couples whose wedding night was filled with frustration, fears, and the shedding of a few tears. More concerning to me are the couples I meet who find themselves disappointed with God because they saved sex for marriage only to have a frustrating sexual experience. It's as though God didn't hold up His end of the bargain.

> We wait, not because of what it will do for us,
> but because of what it will do within us.

But the problem with this entire belief system is that it's rooted in a false claim. We don't wait so we can have an evening of ecstasy on our honeymoon night (because trust me, that's rarely the case). We wait because through the process of waiting our relationship is built, our trust is strengthened, and our commitment to each other is tried, tested, and refined. We wait because through the process of waiting, we learn discipline, self-control, loyalty, and reverence for the sacred. We wait because it's an act of worship and obedience to a God who knows exactly how we're wired, what we need, and what is best for our lives. Our waiting is an act of trusting, and trusting God always leads us to greater things. We wait, not because of what it will do for us, but because of what it will do within us. Because you can't estab-lish a good sex life until you've established good character first.

## Married Sex 101

I know a couple who spent the day after their wedding at a book-store, buying and then reading all the books they could find about how to have sex. And they're not alone in their lack of knowledge—they were just courageous enough to admit it and then do something about it. A huge part of the problem is that within the Christian culture at large, the majority of what we're taught about sex before marriage is wrapped up in three familiar words: "Don't do it." We treat sex like a say-no-to-drugs campaign, and then somehow, suddenly, once we're married, we're supposed to just do it and do it well. We assume we'll know exactly what to do, and without much effort it will be incredible. But typically, that's not the case.

Not only that, but the influence of culture, through things like the entertainment industry, pornography, and the hookup culture, leaves us with knowledge about sex that's neither accurate nor healthy. We're receiving an overload of messages about sex from the world, yet hearing very little about it from the church. It's a topic that's rarely discussed from the pulpit. But in our silence, we're conveying a message. Ironically, by not saying anything about sex, we *are* saying something. We're saying it's a topic that's not supposed to be talked about. Unfortunately, many couples carry that view of sex into marriage. And in the silence, our views of sex and sexuality are shaped and molded, yet with no gauge of what's healthy or good. I have worked with far too many couples who have not fully enjoyed sex within marriage because they have never learned how. In many cases, it's not a lack of intimacy or love that drives an unsatisfied sex life; it's a lack of understanding.

### Practice Makes Perfect

> It's a process of becoming a better person as much as it is about becoming a better lover.

They say good sex starts in the kitchen, and it does. What's meant by this is that it's not in the bedroom, but in the everyday interactions with each other that our sex lives begin to grow, to form, and to take shape. Through marriage you learn that sex isn't this one-time action in the heat of the moment like the Hollywood movies tend to portray. Real-life sex in its intended form is a process. It's a process of learning selflessness, trust, communication, and a whole lot of grace. It's a process of learning to be vulnerable, asking for what we need and trusting our spouse to meet us where we are. It's a process of becoming a better person as much as it is about becoming a better lover.

The framework of marriage is the one and only way we get to watch this process unfold in the most meaningful way: the process of becoming healthy, becoming whole, and becoming one throughout a lifetime. There's a lot to learn about having a healthy sex life. It's an ongoing process, not something you can figure all out on your wedding night. I look back at our honeymoon and I have to chuckle a bit. As I shared before, it was quite a learning curve, filled with laughs, trial and error, and a whole lot of practice. But practice makes perfect, and I have to say I am honored to have the chance to practice with this man I love so deeply for the rest of our lives. That's what marital sex is all about. Over a decade into marriage and our sex life gets better and better with each passing year. And I look forward to the many years we have to continue learning, growing, and enjoying each other through this God-given gift of marital sex.

Just like anything significant in life, good sex takes time, energy, and understanding to get better. And it's so worth it! I hear from older couples who are investing in their relationship and thriving in their marriage that their sex life always follows suit—getting healthier, happier, and more exciting along the way. I recently met a couple in their sixties who said their sex life is the best it's ever been. The honeymoon was simply the start, the beginning of the journey. It's important for us to have healthy expectations of this thing called sex long before we enter a marriage relationship, because those very beliefs will either propel us forward or keep us stagnant when the problem spots come along.

## Sex Marks the Spot

Going into marriage, no one imagines they'll face problem spots in their sex life. But according to a survey I took of over 1000 married people, almost 80 percent of married couples encounter sexual struggles at some point in their marriage. I asked them to tell me about the most common sexual struggles they've faced. Out of all the answers that came in, two problem spots stood out, yet are hardly talked about.

### Problem Spot #1: Difference in Sexual Desire (or a lack of desire altogether):

A thread about a man who kept a detailed spreadsheet recording all the times his wife denied him sex within a 44-day span went totally viral on Reddit.[1] The spreadsheet was broken down into three columns: the date, sex? (yes or no), and the excuse. In a span of 44 days that included 27 requests for sex, his wife said yes to sex only three times. In the 24 times she said no, he recorded her responses, listing phrases such as "I'm watching the show," "I have to be up early," or "I'm too tired." When the post went viral, it perpetuated the stereotype that this is often how married sex goes.

But are these stereotypes valid? Is this pattern true within a marriage? Is it typical for a man to have a higher sexual desire than a woman? Does married sex have to end in a spreadsheet that records a pattern of perpetual rejection? Well, yes and no. There's no easy answer to the reality of differences in sexual desire, but there are certainly ways to navigate this problem spot that don't include keeping a depressing spreadsheet.

Let's start with the basics. We can certainly affirm that, generally speaking, males tend to have a higher sex drive than females. A review of the scientific literature confirmed that "across many different studies and measures, men have been shown to have more frequent and more intense sexual desires than women."[2] While we can certainly see evidence that males have a higher sexual drive than women, we must be careful not to paint broad brushstrokes that apply to every marriage. Each marriage is different, because it's made up of two unique people with unique needs and desires. In some marriages, the woman may have a higher sexual drive, and in other marriages, the man. But often, sexual drive ebbs and flows throughout a marriage. There are peaks and there are valleys, but the main thing to understand is that there's a good chance your peak is going to coincide with your partner's valley at some point in your marriage. In my survey of over 1000 married people, over 61 percent reported that differences in sexual desire, or a lack of desire altogether, was the number-one struggle they faced in their sexual relationship.

So how often is the average married couple having sex? People often wonder about the answer to that question, yet it's not a subject you bring up with your friends at Sunday brunch. For my own curiosity, I had to include this question on the survey as well. I found it interesting to note that even with the reported differences in desire, most married couples (44.7%) reported having sex 1–2 times a week on average. But interesting to note, the next largest group (26.6%) reported having sex 1–2 times per *month* on average. There seems to be quite a difference between couples and what they consider the norm. The rest of the bunch (the last 28.7%, to whom we'll refer as the outliers) were evenly split at either far above the average (3–4 times a week, or even daily), or way below average (meaning, they don't remember the last time they had sex, or they're unable to have traditional intercourse because of physical limitations).

In looking at all the data that came in regarding sex in marriage and taking into consideration the different stories I've heard along the way in both my personal and clinical experience, I can conclusively say there's no one-size-fits-all formula for what sex should look like within a marriage. We are likely going to deal with differences in sexual desires and needs, but we're going to face them in a different way than the couple next door. Yet while every couple's struggles might look a little different, their strategies to overcome those struggles should look similar. Let me offer some strategies to give you a start in dealing with differences in sexual desire.

## COMMUNICATE WITH YOUR SPOUSE

When you're struggling with differences in sexual desire, it can cause a major emotional rift in your marriage. Jessica and Ben were a couple who found themselves having argument after argument about this very thing late into the night. Jessica was struggling with hormonal changes and exhaustion after the birth of their third child, and all she wanted at the end of the day was to get some rest. Ben's version of resting, on the other hand, was the thought of being intimate with his wife. Jessica didn't want to force it, or feel like she "had to" have sex with him. Ben couldn't wrap his brain around the fact that she wasn't in the mood. Their difference in desire and perspective often led them to argue, going to bed with Jessica feeling uncared for and Ben feeling rejected. For the person on the receiving end of the lack of interest, it's easy to interpret the difference in desire as rejection.

But before jumping to the conclusion that the difference in desire is purely rejection or selfishness, it's important to take the time to interact with your spouse and find out what's going on behind the scenes. While it's easy to put up walls and go to bed feeling frustrated, we must see these moments as opportunities to build bridges, understand our spouses a little bit better, and together find solutions. When Jessica and Ben were finally willing to communicate about their needs, Ben discovered that Jessica was simply feeling drained from a long day's work with three children. She needed Ben to step in with the children and the house in ways that would free her to save her energy for "after hours." Ben communicated to Jessica that intimacy was his way of feeling emotionally and physically connected to his wife. After a long day of getting beat up by the world, he needed his wife's affirmation and acceptance. When they each expressed their needs and perspectives, they understood each other better and could make choices that took the other into consideration. Ben started to take seriously his duty to help around the house and with the kids, and Jessica started to see sex not as a duty, but as an act of love, offering affirmation and security to her husband.

And this scenario certainly goes both ways. Sometimes holding on to the stereotype that men always want sex can cause some major harm in a marriage relationship. In some seasons the wife will have a stronger desire for sex than the husband. I know of many women who found themselves struggling with insecurities and entertaining unfounded fears because their husbands weren't as interested in sex as they were. One woman who comes to mind started feeling a deep sense of anxiety whenever her husband failed to initiate sex. Rather than discuss it with him, she called me in a panic, wondering if maybe he was cheating on her or getting his sexual needs met in another way. But a healthy sex life is always built on healthy communication, and I encouraged her to share her concerns and desires with her husband. He explained to her that he had been working extra hours for the past few months and he was feeling especially stressed and tired. His lack of initiation wasn't a lack of desire; simply put, it was a lack of energy. Talking about it was the first step in bringing them closer, helping her to see life from his perspective and put her insecurities to rest. Then they could move forward, considering each other's needs and finding the right balance between much-needed sleep and much-needed intimacy.

It's important to remember that every marriage is unique. But you can't *consider* the other until you *understand* the other, which is why communication is such an important part of this process.

## Learn About Your Spouse

Let me ask you this: how much have you learned about sex? And I don't mean "learned from experience." I mean learned from a credible resource (Googling it doesn't count). The sad reality is that so often, part of the reason couples are struggling in their sexual lives is a lack of proper education and awareness of the subject. Have you ever read a good book about sex in marriage? Do you have a healthy understanding of the male/female anatomy and sexual differences? Are you knowledgeable about how to make the sexual experience the best it can be for your spouse? If you want to increase desire, you need to start by increasing understanding. Learn about what makes your spouse tick from both an anatomical perspective as well as from an emotional/spiritual perspective. Our sexual needs are tied to our emotional needs, and the more you can learn about your spouse, the better you can please them. And it goes the other way too, in that the more you can "teach" your spouse about you, the better the experience will be for both of you.

In one of my favorite books about sex, *Sheet Music*, Dr. Kevin Leman compares the process of learning about sex to the process of learning to play an instrument.

> If I handed you a violin and said, "Play it," you'd proba-
> bly say to me, "I can't play the violin." But if I insisted—
> "Come on, I want you to play it"—you might at least give
> it a try. If you're like most people picking up the violin
> for the first time, you'd make a rather awkward sound, at
> which point I would say, "Good, that's good!" My guess
> is that you'd look back at me and say, "Good? That's ter-
> rible! I told you I can't play the violin." "Yes," I'd say, "but
> you made noise, and that's just the beginning." Getting
> started with your sex life is much the same as learning a
> new musical instrument. What you need to do is learn
> how to make music—your job is to create a symphony
> with your [spouse]...great sex takes time to perfect.[3]

In learning how to achieve great sex, communication is going to come into play again, because in the process of learning there's got to be an openness and honesty regarding the sexual experience. Because men and women are wired so differently anatomically, there has to be an open discussion about what feels good and what doesn't. What are you comfortable with, and what would you rather not do? What gets you going, and what brings you to a complete halt? Don't ever assume that what works for you is going to work for your spouse. Because maybe, just maybe, part of the difference in sexual desire is a difference in how you each desire sex. And remember that what felt good yesterday, is not necessarily going to feel good today. We're constantly changing in our bodies and needs, and with that in mind there should be an ongoing conversation with this goal in mind: to learn how to share your sexual needs as well as how to best please your spouse. Sex isn't a duty; it's a process of discovery. And the more you know about your spouse, the better you'll do (and the more fun it will be!).

## Give to Your Spouse

In healthy sex, there can and should be just as much pleasure in giving as there is in receiving. The Song of Solomon (or the Song of Songs in some translations) is an intimate look into a healthy sex life. One theme that continually stands out to me is the ongoing give-and-take throughout the book between the husband and wife. Two people, passionately giving of themselves to please the other, without reservation. "Let my beloved come to his garden, and eat its choicest fruits" (Song of Solomon 4:16 ESV). In this passage, the woman doesn't even refer to her body as her own, but as her beloved's. Calling it "his garden," she sends a clear and deliberate message that sex in marriage is not just about the taking, but the giving.

Like everything in marriage, sex is an act of service more than an act of being served. Part of the process of enjoying sex is learning to take pleasure in our spouse's enjoyment. That kind of giving attitude must start outside of the bedroom, and it works its way into the bedroom. When each spouse can set their heart's desires on serving and loving the other, the sexual end result will be mind-blowing. The best sex is an interaction that sets its goal on pleasing rather than simply being pleased.

This is why shallow things like pornography, compulsive masturbation, and even extramarital affairs can never hold a candle to the incredible intimacy that comes from the give-and-take of a good marriage. Those types of things are determined to do one thing and one thing only: take. They're a one-way street when it comes to pleasure, because the focus is not on giving, but only on taking. But God, in His sovereignty, has *created* us to be a people who take pleasure in giving, just as much (if not more!) as we do in receiving.

Paul refers to this incredible mystery when he references the words of Jesus that affirm the reality that a person is "far happier giving than getting" (Acts 20:35 MSG). This passage can apply to many different areas of life, and it certainly applies to sex. Those who can make it their goal to serve their spouse sexually will find their desire is not linked to their personal needs in the moment, but rather is most in tune to the needs of their spouse. Two people, each giving their very best for their spouse...What a marvelous place to be in the give-and-take of marriage.

### Problem Spot #2: A Lack of Physical Attraction

Have you ever felt a lack of physical attraction to your spouse? I asked that question in a survey of over 1000 married people. What would you guess was the percentage of people who answered yes to that question versus those who answered no? I then asked that same question of singles, but this time I asked them to predict what they thought was the percentage of married people who reported feeling a lack of physical attraction toward their spouse. The vast majority of singles got the answer *wrong*, assuming a lack of physical attraction hardly happened in a healthy marriage. But in actuality, 50 percent of married people admitted struggling with a lack of physical attraction toward their spouse at some point in their marriage. I find it concerning that not many people are teaching about or addressing this issue so that such a large number of people are struggling with it. And I would venture to say that this percentage would likely increase if these very same people were polled again with the passing of time and the increasing of age.

Let's get real. When it comes to physical attraction, *ain't none of us gonna be lookin' fine* when we're nearing 80 years old. As each year passes, I'm growing increasingly aware of the limits of my physical body. My good looks are only going to carry me so far in life. With the passing of time comes a scattering of gray hairs, the creasing of new wrinkles, a few stubborn extra pounds, and a little more sagging of this and of that. And this is only the beginning. Within the past decade of marriage, my husband has witnessed me at my worst, not only emotionally but physically. He's seen the crazy hair moments, the bad breath moments, the morning-sickness-vomiting-in-the-toilet moments, the messy-delivering-a-baby moments, and every not-so-appealing moment in between. We have seen each other at our absolute worst, which is both the reality and privilege of two human beings living under one roof for a lifetime.

The ebbs and flows of physical attraction are a normal part of the marriage experience. And to me, they are not concerning because a good marriage is made up of so much more than the physical. In those moments when physical attraction may find itself on the back burner, what holds a strong marriage together is every other attraction two people have built along the way: the emotional, the spiritual, the relational, the mental. The magnetic force of commitment, time, and experience all wrapped up into one can bring a couple together in a way that no one but God could think of.

Maybe some of you are in a stage of life where you have lost sight of the many things that hold you and your spouse together. Maybe you're struggling to find an attraction, and it's starting to have an impact on your sexual relationship. I counseled a young man who was having a hard time finding that physical spark toward his wife. He found himself dwelling on the physical attributes she was lacking, or comparing her to the other women he would see. He felt a terrible guilt about it and sought help to alleviate this struggle he was facing. I shared with him three big picture themes I address with couples who are dealing with a lack of physical attraction, and I want to share them with you as well.

## Your Mind

*Disciplines of the Beautiful Woman* is an insightful book from several decades ago by Anne Ortlund. Throughout that book, Anne refers to the power of focus in the process of ordering our lives, from managing time all the way to organizing a closet and everything in between. She uses the phrase "concentrate and eliminate."[4] She talks about the importance of prioritizing the good things and the important things, and then getting rid of all the rest. That term has stuck with me over the years, and I've found myself applying it to practically everything. One area where this phrase has come in handy has been in the context of "ordering" our sexual lifestyles and habits.

When it comes to our sexual lives, the things we give our time, our thoughts, and our energy to are what will grow, while the things we neglect to invest in will naturally wither. This can be a great thing or a terrible thing, depending on what we choose to focus on. To grasp this concept, let's compare our sexual preferences to taste. I remember the first time I tasted dark chocolate. It tasted terrible to me as a child. It was so bad that I spit it out. At the time, my palate couldn't handle the rich taste of the pure cocoa flavor. Compared to the sugared-up, milk-loaded version of "chocolate" I was used to, this "real" stuff tasted like dirt. It wasn't until I was older that my palate began to change, as I was exposed to more and more of the "good stuff." For any hope of enjoying dark chocolate, I had to "concentrate and eliminate," per se. Years later, I would now consider myself to be a dark chocolate connoisseur (just writing this chapter reminded me it was time for a dark chocolate break). It's so incredibly delicious. And the darker, the better. I am just thrilled when John brings me home a bar made of 70 percent or even 80 percent pure cacao. Now I can hardly stand the taste of regular milk chocolate, which is an anomaly around here, considering we live so close to the milk chocolate capital of the world: Hershey, Pennsylvania. My palate has done a complete 180.

When it comes to our sexual palates, something similar occurs behind the scenes in our brains. Our sexual palates are shaped and molded based on what we've been exposed to in the past, as well as what we expose ourselves to along the way. The more we fill our minds with junk like pornography and explicit movies and novels, the more we'll be enslaved to those unrealistic sexual expectations, and in turn, sabotage our most intimate relationships. As it's often said, junk in equals junk out.

But let me be clear. This is not just about disciplining our minds by saying no to overt trash, but also about learning to discipline our minds even when faced with the day-to-day opportunities for lust and temptation. What kind of entertainment are we integrating into our way of thinking? What does our Netflix movie queue tell us about the way we view sex and relationships? What level of discipline do we have over our thought life when given the opportunity to take a second look at that scantily dressed "body" working out next to us at the gym? In Scripture, Mark 9:47 encourages us to take inventory of anything that's causing us to sin, and remove it from our lives. Is there anything we need to cut out of our lives in order to move toward sexual integrity? The discipline of our minds requires us to ask the hard questions and then dig deep for the answers to get ourselves to a better place. That's how we stop sin in its tracks: by learning to concentrate on the good and eliminate all else from our lives.

Back to the young man I mentioned above. His sexual palate was taking shape without him realizing it, right there in his mind, based on what he was allowing himself to dwell on and look at. For his sexual palate to start changing, and his attraction toward his wife to grow, he had to learn to concentrate (on the positive attributes of his wife) and eliminate all the things that were inhibiting him (pornography, lustful thoughts, checking out other women). He had to take all his sexual thoughts and energy and concentrate only on his wife, the woman God had blessed him with. God's Word affirms this idea by challenging us to "take every thought captive to obey Christ" (2 Corinthians 10:5 esv). What a beautiful picture of taking control of the things that might hinder us and hold us back. Our thought life is so important, and God's Word continually affirms its power. Another verse that comes to mind is Philippians 4:8, which highlights the importance of deliberately concentrating on that which is good:

> Whatever is true, whatever is honorable, whatever is just, whatever is pure, whatever is lovely, whatever is commendable, if there is any excellence, if there is anything worthy of praise, think about these things (esv).

As the young man in the story above began to eliminate the bad and concentrate on the good, his attraction toward his wife began to grow anew, and his desire for her began to take shape all over again.

## (To Me) You Are Flawless

One thing I especially love about the Song of Solomon is the way the couple spends time "concentrating" on the good in each other. Both the lover and the beloved spend verse after verse going back and forth, simply describing in detail the things they love about each other.

> Bride:
>
> Let him kiss me with the kisses of his mouth! For your love is better than wine...As an apple tree among the trees of the forest, so is my beloved among the young men. With great delight I sat in his shadow, and his fruit was sweet to my taste...My beloved is like a gazelle or a young stag...Arise, my love, my beautiful one, and come away. O my dove, in the clefts of the rock, in the crannies of the cliff, let me see your face, let me hear your voice, for your

voice is sweet, and your face is lovely (Song of Solomon
1:2; 2:3,9,13-14 ESV).

Groom:

Behold, you are beautiful, my love, behold, you are beautiful! Your eyes are doves behind your veil. Your hair is like
a flock of goats leaping down the slopes of Gilead. Your
teeth are like a flock of shorn ewes that have come up
from the washing, all of which bear twins, and not one
among them has lost its young. Your lips are like a scar-
let thread, and your mouth is lovely. Your cheeks are like
halves of a pomegranate behind your veil. Your neck is
like the tower of David, built in rows of stone; on it hang a
thousand shields, all of them shields of warriors. Your two
breasts are like two fawns, twins of a gazelle, that graze
among the lilies. Until the day breathes and the shad-
ows flee, I will go away to the mountain of myrrh and
the hill of frankincense. You are altogether beautiful, my
love; there is no flaw in you (Song of Solomon 4:1-7 ESV).

I love that the groom ends that section by declaring to his bride
that "there is no flaw in you." To him, she was simply flawless. If she
was anything like the average real-life woman (and men, this can
apply to you too), she probably struggled to believe that about herself.
I was perusing the latest fashions at a clothing store recently, when I
came upon a series of shirts with the word FLAWLESS printed on them
in bright, bold colors. I guess you could attribute it to my personal
insecurities, but I found myself wondering who on earth would wear
a shirt declaring that they're flawless. I sure wouldn't. I could easily
think of a few things I'd consider "flaws" within myself. And I have a
feeling this young bride felt the same way.

At the start of the book, she comments about her skin and explains
that she really hasn't had the opportunity to take care of herself the
way she would have liked: "My own vineyard I have not kept!" (Song

of Solomon 1:6 ESV). Based on the previous picture she paints of herself, I have a feeling that if you lined up the most beautiful women in her region, this hard-working Shulammite girl would likely not have made the top of the list. There's a good chance she struggled to feel worthy, attractive, and desirable. But in one bold statement, the groom affirms that there is no one he wants more, calling her the "most beautiful among women." Her groom chose to focus on no one but her. She was the only one he chose to see, and the only one he wanted. His concentration was set on his bride, and his satisfaction in her was above all else.

Imagine if we apply that same drive and focus, that same "concentration," to the way we view our spouse? I mean, what would happen if we consistently zoom in on their strengths, talents, and character, and speak them out loud? What if we simply appreciate them for who they are, rather than dwell on who we want them to be? This doesn't just apply to our physical attraction and sex lives; it applies to every aspect of our marriages. Concentrate on the good, eliminate the bad, and you'll find your marital connection achieving heights you never imagined.

## YOUR BODY

Another important step toward rekindling physical attraction in marriage is taking inventory of your physical health as a couple. Now, I just so happen to be writing this portion of the book on my birthday. In the past, I've approached birthdays with much excitement and anticipation, but this birthday has been a little harder to swallow. As joyous as it has been celebrating God's faithfulness in my life, and as grateful as I am for the life and family He's given me, this birthday has also come with a mixture of emotions. This last year, I faced a few difficult and unexpected health issues that sort of shook me up. Thankfully, those health concerns have come and gone, but the reality of getting older paired with my awareness of the limitations of my physical health have opened my eyes to the importance of taking care of my body in a way I've never considered before.

We often apply 1 Corinthians 6:20 ("Honor God with your bodies") to our spiritual and emotional decisions, but fail to apply it to our physical decisions as well. What we eat and drink as well as how we invest in our physical health and well-being are all decisions that can be used to honor God with our bodies, or not. An insightful article I read at DesiringGod.com refers to gluttony as "America's most tolerated sin."[5] I, for one, find myself convicted by that title. The important thing to grasp is that even something as basic as considering what (or how much) we eat and drink is an opportunity to bring glory to God (1 Corinthians 10:31 ESV). But not only are we honoring God when we choose to invest in our personal health; we're honoring our spouse by giving them the best version of ourselves.

This is so much more important than simply trying to achieve a certain weight or a specific clothing size. It's not about that at all. It's about health, and wholeness, and learning the discipline of striving to do the best we can with what we've been given. Something about taking responsibility for our health in this way is truly appealing and attractive, because it shows we care. In a way, our physical health and well-being are a gift we give to ourselves as well as to our spouse.

A friend of mine watched this conviction take root in her husband's heart a few years after they were married. He was an incredible man who also tended to be incredibly unhealthy. She was genuinely concerned for his health and well-being, and so she committed to praying for him, encouraging him, and supporting him. A few years into their marriage, he had a health scare that triggered his desire for change. He started simple: cutting out the sugary drinks and being more aware about what he ate throughout the day. He eventually added exercise and learned the discipline of moderation. Within one year, both his health and appearance had completely transformed, and he felt so much better than he'd ever felt before. He gave his wife the precious gift of himself—healthy, whole, and strong. And as a result of his physical health, their sex life got healthier. As any medical doctor or therapist will tell you, the two often go hand in hand.[6]

When it comes to the correlation of physical attraction in marriage and physical health, I believe it's important for each one of us to take inventory of where we are with how we care for our bodies and the impact it may be having on our sex lives. A few of us might be able to say we eat well, exercise frequently, get regular checkups, and keep our bodies in great condition. But if the rest of us were honest with ourselves, we'd likely admit we have much room for improvement. There's no better time than the present to take those next steps in getting your physical health to a better place.

But maybe you're on the other side of this equation, married to someone who's not motivated to get healthy. You might be worried about their health or even struggling with your level of attraction toward them. My advice is to first check your heart (read below) and then, as your spouse is willing, tackle this issue together with heaps of encouragement, prayer, and support. Criticism and shaming have no role in the equation of getting healthy. They often deplete motivation and drive a wedge between you and your spouse, leaving you each feeling more helpless than before. Instead, work together to set achievable goals, integrate exercise into your time together, and strive to create healthy menus you can accomplish as a team. Keep each other encouraged and accountable as you move toward a place of honoring both God and each other with how you care for your bodies.

## Your Heart

At the end of the day, the best thing you can do for your sexual relationship is to get your heart right. Sometimes in marriage, a lack of attraction has absolutely nothing to do with the person standing before you, and everything to do with your own heart. It's so easy to get fixated on what your spouse is lacking (physically, emotionally, or sexually), when instead you should be focused on asking God to reveal to you what may be lacking in your own heart.

> Ongoing attraction has far less to do with
> the desirability of our spouse and far more
> to do with the condition of our heart.

Maybe you're holding on to bitterness or resentment. It could be you've allowed your emotional connection to take a backseat, and now it's beginning to affect your physical connection. Maybe your spouse is doing something that's bothering or hurting you, but rather than communicate, you've chosen to hold back. It could be you're clinging to unrealistic or unhealthy expectations of what sex should look like in marriage. Maybe you've allowed the seed of unforgiveness to take root in your heart. Maybe your sexual history is creeping its way in and having a negative impact on your intimacy. Or maybe you're playing the comparison game, holding your spouse up to a measuring stick of something—or *someone*—else, by which they were never meant to be measured.

In his book *Cherish*, Gary Thomas refers to a prayer he prayed early on in his marriage that reflects the importance of a right heart within the context of marital attraction: "Lord, let my wife define beautiful to me. Let her be the standard for what I find most attractive."[7] Gary goes on to say that God answered this prayer. And after 31 years of marriage, his standard of beauty is defined by nothing less than his wife. To him, she is the only standard. She is his "plumb line" of beauty. That type of ongoing attraction has far less to do with the desirability of our spouse and far more to do with the condition of our heart.

For you today, maybe this begins with a prayer similar to Gary's. Or maybe it begins with asking the Lord to reveal to you the things in your life you need to let go of or change as you begin the process of moving toward your spouse. In the pursuit of getting our hearts right, we need to get to a place where, just like David, we can boldly and courageously plead, "Create in me a clean heart, O God, and renew a right spirit within me" (Psalm 51:10 ESV). Is anything inside of your heart keeping you from feeling a meaningful attraction toward your spouse? If so, it's time to recognize it, acknowledge it, and then take the necessary steps toward overcoming it. Even in the bedroom, this kind of attitude will be the only thing that can take your sex life from *me* to *we*.

## Your Sexual Appetite

Allow me to take a moment to address the singles reading this chapter. I know, I know. You just read an entire chapter about marital sex. But don't worry. I haven't forgotten about you. The whole idea of having a "sexual appetite" is such an important concept to grasp long before you get married, because the sexual appetite you have before you enter marriage will be the sexual appetite you bring into marriage. Your sexual palate is being shaped and formed with everything you allow yourself to be exposed to and everything you take into your mind, your body, and your heart. It's important to take inventory of any harmful things that may be having a negative impact on the way you desire and perceive sex. Seek accountability to get yourself out of the pit of pornography use. Get a tight rein on your thought life. Stop feeding your mind entertainment that will pollute it with lust and sexual images. Prune out all that is harmful and replace it with healthy interactions with the community of people God has placed in your life. And if you don't have a community, it's time to turn off Netflix, get off social media, and start investing in real-life relationships with godly people. The people you surround yourself with will influence the kind of person you become. It's time to get plugged in to your local church and ministry and start taking control of the shaping of your heart, long before you say "I do."

## From Infatuation to Adoration

On the day of your wedding, you will find yourself at the absolute peak of infatuation. But if you're imagining a mountain-shaped graph, with infatuation peaking at the top of the triangle, you might find yourself disappointed at the imagery that it's only downhill from there. If you define infatuation as the height of emotion and attraction, then that is a rather depressing thought, isn't it? But that's absolutely *not* what I am saying. The fact that infatuation fades is only disappointing for those of you who believe infatuation is the best of all emotions in marriage. I'm here to tell you that it's not. Not even close.

> If infatuation is fueled by the mystery of the unknown, adoration is fueled by the intimacy of the known.

The best is yet to come. There's something far more significant than infatuation: adoration. If infatuation is fueled by the mystery of the unknown, adoration is fueled by the intimacy of the known. It's the beautiful connection between two people who know each other deeply and love each other still. It's the indescribable feeling of having your heart, mind, spirit, and body on display, yet knowing that you're loved fiercely. It's being aware of the flaws within your spouse, yet choosing to love anyway. Adoration isn't fueled by emotion; it's fueled by choice. And no matter how exhausted, disappointed, frustrated, or insecure you are, adoration always makes a point of raising the needs of your spouse higher than your own. It always chooses one thing and one thing alone. It always chooses marriage.

My prayer for each of you reading this book today is that God will move you past the superficial emotion of infatuation and challenge you to live in a place of deliberate adoration. And that in the process of bettering your sex lives, you will find something even more valuable: the bettering of your heart.

# REFLECTION QUESTIONS
# FOR MARRIED COUPLES

1. Remembering the honeymoon story at the start of this chapter, what would you say is the difference between your expectations of sex before marriage and the reality of sex within your marriage? Take some time to think that through and discuss.

2. What has been the greatest sexual struggle you've faced within marriage? In what ways has this struggle affected your relationship with each other?

3. What is the current frequency of your sexual intimacy? Discuss this together and answer the following questions:

   a. What do you enjoy most about your sexual life?

   b. What would you like to do differently/change regarding your sexual life?

   c. What are some obstacles that can get in the way of a fulfilling sex life?

   d. What are some things you can do to enhance your sexual life?

# REFLECTION QUESTIONS
# FOR SINGLES

1. In what ways is your "sexual appetite" being shaped at this point in your life?

2. Do you need to "eliminate" any actions, behaviors, entertainment, or relationships to begin transforming your sexual palate during this time of singleness?

3. Is your current thought life contributing to a healthy view of sex or an unhealthy view of sex? (Reread Philippians 4:8 and 2 Corinthians 10:5.) In what ways can you practically begin to "take every thought captive" and start dwelling on that which is "pure and good"?

# Better Together

*From Independence to Oneness*

Many people believe they have fallen in love, only to realize their "love" is based on need—a need to be wanted, a need to be valued, a need to be affirmed. A need to be taken care of, to be nurtured, to be kept safe. "Need love" drives you toward someone out of desperation, insecurities, and fear. It fools an empty person into thinking this relationship can somehow fill them up. But in the end, fulfillment never comes. In the end, their desperate need causes them to feel more and more depleted and more and more alone. In the end, their needs grow even greater in the shadow of a false and dying love.

I counseled a young woman who was struggling in this type of marriage relationship. She was so desperate for a relationship that she jumped into marriage long before she was emotionally or psychologically ready. She was emotionally and spiritually empty, yet subconsciously hoping that this man would be the very thing that would fill her up. They were both Christians, and they were both in love—certainly that would be enough, she convinced herself. But day after day her insecurities and needs began to grow. As much as her husband tried, he couldn't seem to do enough to get her to a better place.

She was desperate for more, and the moment marriage wasn't filling her up she would find herself disillusioned and disappointed. Marriage had failed her, she thought. God had failed her, she blamed. But maybe, just maybe, she had failed herself.

"Need love" takes root in the hearts of men and women long before they get married. It's birthed out of feeling incomplete, unfulfilled, and inadequate while standing alone. It's rooted in the false assumption that a relationship will "fill me up" and complete that missing piece. Too many people go into marriage hoping it will complete them, only to be gravely disappointed in the end. Because while marriage can certainly add so much to your life, it will never be able to fill you up. You can feel only as complete in a marriage as you do while standing alone.

## Codependence Is Not Oneness

The word *codependence* comes up a lot in my sessions as a professional counselor. While the term was originally used to describe the spouses of alcoholics, the traits of codependence began to be observed in many other relationships with an unhealthy reliance on one spouse by the other. It was eventually referred to as a "relationship addiction," because it was seen in individuals who would do just about anything to maintain a relationship, no matter how unhealthy, toxic, one-sided, or abusive that relationship was.

In identifying a dependent personality, a counselor is often looking for these specific traits outlined by the DSM-V:[1]

- Has difficulty making everyday decisions without an excessive amount of advice and reassurance from others.

- Needs others to assume responsibility for most major areas of his or her life.

- Has difficulty expressing disagreement with others because of fear of loss of support or approval.

- Has difficulty initiating projects or doing things on his or her own (because of a lack of self-confidence in judgment or abilities rather than a lack of motivation or energy).

- Goes to excessive lengths to obtain nurturance and support from others, to the point of volunteering to do things that are unpleasant.

- Feels uncomfortable or helpless when alone because of exaggerated fears of being unable to care for himself or herself.

- Urgently seeks another relationship as a source of care and support when a close relationship ends.

- Is unrealistically preoccupied with fears of being left to take care of himself or herself.

> Codependent people usually come from backgrounds of pain, hurt, neglect, rejection, abandonment, or abuse, and somewhere along the way they believed the lie that they need to prove they are worth loving.

Codependent people look to others for approval, for affirmation, for validation, and even for worth. They are drawn into relationships because of what they "need" rather than what they have to give. Being alone is almost impossible, because they need people to feel affirmed and valuable. Codependent people usually come from backgrounds of pain, hurt, neglect, rejection, abandonment, or abuse, and somewhere along the way they believed the lie that they need to prove they are worth loving. The part I find most fascinating is that many of these traits are seen within the context of Christian relationships, but often fail to be identified. Some of these very characteristics are perpetuated and unknowingly encouraged.

I was recently visiting a Christian college for a speaking engagement when one young woman came up to me for a chat after my talk. She was rather perplexed hearing me share the concept that a relationship can't complete you. She had been raised to believe that getting married was the only way to fulfill her God-given purpose, and that becoming one with her future husband would complete the big picture of the meaning of her life. This is the very problem I see. Far too many people mistake the concept of *codependence* with oneness, yet they are so completely opposite! Codependence proclaims *I'm desperate without you*, whereas oneness affirms *I'm better with you*. The former is based on getting what we lack; the latter is rooted in what we have to give.

We all struggle with the negative characteristics of codependence at times. We long for approval, we desire affirmation, and we often aim to please others even at the expense of our values and beliefs. It's a constant struggle to make sure we're living for "an audience of one" (God), rather than living to simply please those around us. Part of that is the natural struggle of being human and being created for relationships. We're all needy in some way, because we're ultimately in need of a Savior. A Savior who can bind up our wounds, speak value and worth into our lives, and fill us to overflowing with His love. But if we're not careful, we can quickly find ourselves slipping into a place where approval from others begins to be prioritized higher than approval from God.

## The Lie of Independence

But then there are those on the opposite end of the spectrum. Out of a fear of relying on or trusting others, they glorify independence instead. They refuse to ask for help or share their needs in any way because they falsely believe there is strength in managing alone. I got an email from a young woman trying to figure out the balancing act of accepting help in a culture that tends to promote independence above all else. "As a 28-year-old single woman, I want to be independent. But it's often a burden. For example, I recently needed something fixed in my apartment but couldn't get myself to ask a male friend at church out of the fear of looking needy."

We live in a culture that really relishes that way of thinking, encouraging us to trust no one, believe no one, need no one. Yet that way of thinking leaves us completely isolated and alone, depending on ourselves as the be-all and end-all. The important thing to realize about this characteristic is that it's deceiving. It gives the appearance of control, but it's typically found in people who feel or have felt a lack of control in some area of their life. Those who fall under the category of "complete and total independence" have a deep-seated belief that they don't need people. But often that lack of need stems from an inability to trust others to do for them. *What if they don't come through? What if they let me down? What if they don't do it the way I want it done?* This mentality can be harmful when carried over into relationships. Couples completely independent from each other continue to function as individuals, even within the context of a relationship, each making decisions, plans, and preparations for only themselves and expecting their partner to do the same. This type of unhealthy independence offers the illusion of strength, but is often rooted in deep fears, insecurities, weaknesses, and a paralyzing inability to trust.

## Marry Someone Who Makes You Better: Interdependence

If codependence tips you toward one side of an unhealthy relationship, and complete independence tips you toward the other, then how on earth does a person engage in a healthy marriage? Well, you walk the middle ground. So much of life is about learning to live in balance, and this aspect of marriage is no different. If one side of the scale is codependence, and the other side is total independence, the middle ground is represented by one of my favorite words: *interdependence*.

In other words, *marry someone who will make you better*. That should be the motto of Christian relationships and the beauty of interdependence. Interdependence is the third characteristic and the one we're all after, because it's balanced, healthy, and strong. According to God's Word, interdependence is the ideal way to look at relationships. It's the perspective that relationships are a part of life, and though we don't *need* one another for value and worth, we *choose* one another because through relationships we're given an opportunity to show God's love. And in doing so, we become better. We were made for relationships by a God who chose to be in relationship with us, a God who chooses to save us, to serve us, and to connect with us out of sheer love. All through Scripture we're told to encourage one another, edify one another, help one another, and be there for one another (1 Thessalonians 5:11). We're called into the give-and-take relationships found in the community of the body of believers. Like the 28-year-old woman in the story above, when we need something, we should be able to ask for it, knowing that we will have the opportunity to bless and serve others when we're called upon as well.

My husband and I choose to rely on each other for so many things in our day-to-day routine. Not out of desperate *need*, but out of our desire for each other. We were both fairly independent people before marriage, and in coming together we've had to learn to "choose" each other, even during the times we don't necessarily "need" each other. I'm someone who likes to be in control, but I've learned that letting go of certain responsibilities is an act of trust and commitment to my spouse. For example, practically speaking, I've totally relinquished the responsibility of managing our finances. I don't *need* John to manage our finances, but I trust him to. He, on the other hand, has basically handed over his schedule to my care. I oversee our family schedule, keep track of who needs to be where and when, and balance our work and family time.

Another example is in our emotional and spiritual lives. After a particularly hard day for one or the other of us, we choose to unwind, process, vent, pray together, and encourage each other. We don't do this out of a desperate *need*. We could choose to deal with the negative emotions of a hard day in so many different ways—in both good ways and not-so-good ways. But we choose to connect out of love, inviting the other person into that intimate place of our hearts. Choosing to love someone is so much more meaningful than needing someone to love.

To unpack this a little more, let me tell you a funny story. A few years ago, John and I were house hunting. I was pregnant at the time, and we started fairly early that day. By one o'clock, I looked at the clock and realized I hadn't eaten or drunk anything for nearly five hours. I was famished! No, I was more than famished. I was *hangry*. You know what I mean by *hangry*, right? The terrible combination of hungry *and* angry? The starving, irritable, frustrated, annoyed, get-me-something-to-eat-right-now-before-I-eat-*you* kind of feeling? I didn't *want* to eat; I *needed* to eat. Like, *now*!

So John started driving around to find the closest restaurant, but there was nothing in sight. After a few very long minutes, I couldn't wait any longer. "Forget the restaurant. Just get me to a gas station!" So we pulled into a WaWa (yeah, it's really called that; it's a Pennsylvania thing), and I went into that gas station and scarfed down the most greasy, disgusting gas-station food ever known to man. At the time, I didn't care. I just needed to eat. And it felt great for a little while. But about 20 minutes after stuffing my face, I was feeling the negative impact of that poor food decision. I felt as nauseated and bloated as can be. I acted out of my *desperate need*, and in the end I paid for it. Being motivated by *need* and motivated by *choice* are two very different things.

*Choosing* each other is so much more valuable and meaningful than *needing* each other.

Marriage comes with similar aspects. From the superficial, like daily chores and home management, to the more significant, like emotional and spiritual needs, over the years there will be moments of giving and times of receiving. There will be the chance to serve and the opportunity to be served. And in the process, you'll learn that *choosing* each other is so much more valuable and meaningful than *needing* each other. This is the mentality that needs to consistently drive our marriage relationships—a mentality that doesn't need the other, yet chooses to rely on them and care for them out of unconditional love, respect, commitment, and honor.

## The Miracle of Oneness

There is something beautiful about achieving interdependence in a marriage. But the truth is interdependence is not unique to marriage. It can be present within our family relationships and even played out in our friendships. But while interdependence can occur in any significant relationship, according to God's Word there is one thing that is completely unique to marriage.

> In the original creation, God made male and female to be together. Because of this, a man leaves father and mother, and in marriage he becomes one flesh with a woman—no longer two individuals, but forming a new unity. Because God created this organic union of the two sexes, no one should desecrate his art by cutting them apart (Mark 10:6-9 MSG).

That is the miracle of oneness and the very thing that sets marriage apart from every other earthly relationship. In marriage, we move from being two separate entities, and somehow, in some way, we become one flesh. I believe this concept of becoming one flesh is a supernatural experience we can't explain nor fully understand. But one thing I know with all my heart is that when two people enter into the covenant of marriage, they can no longer see themselves as *me*, because they have now become *we*. They have been joined together in a way that God alone can do. This is why we take marriage so seriously, and why it's so important to feel "full" standing alone. Marriage is the fusing of two people's lives, hearts, bodies, and minds in the most intimate way. The two become one. It's not something we do; rather, it's a gift we're given. It's a miracle that points us to a much larger story—the story of a God who chose to connect us intimately with Himself (John 17:21).

## Practical Oneness

In oneness, you have two distinct people, leaving behind their respective families of origin with their baggage, their traditions, their beliefs, and their personalities in the process of becoming distinctively their own. It sounds like a simple decision, but as you've read in earlier chapters, becoming one, choosing *we* over *me*, is a process that unfolds one day at a time, one decision at a time. While the supernatural act of becoming one flesh may occur at the time of being wed, the implications of that oneness unfold over a lifetime.

In the joining of two lives, oneness plays out in many practical ways as well. Two become one with regard to finances, friendships, living space, and daily routines. We join our families, we join our time, we join our entire lives. And over the course of life, even things like our personalities, hobbies, tastes, beliefs, opinions, giftings, preferences, and interests begin to gently morph and change as we rub up against the influence of our spouse.

When John and I got married, we found this process of oneness starting to take shape in our lives in very noticeable ways. One area that comes to mind is our spiritual lives. The first church we attended as a married couple, Riverside Community Church, had set aside a few weeks to focus on spiritual gifts. We were all challenged to take a few spiritual gifts inventories to get to know ourselves a little bit better and understand our unique spiritual wiring. Out of the list of spiritual gifts, my dominant gifts are evangelism and teaching (Romans 12:6-8; Ephesians 4:11). John's dominant gifts are generosity and faith (Romans 12:6-8; 1 Corinthians 12:9). Through our marriage, our unique personalities and giftings have rubbed up against each other in such a way that we've slowly begun to not only appreciate, but to also apply the other's spiritual giftings in our own lives.

I remember the days of John's medical school and my graduate school training, when we were financially living on next to nothing. John's passion and zeal for generosity, giving, and tithing opened my eyes to a new world of giving out of the little we had, having faith to trust that when we gave as God called us to give, He would provide for our needs. John pushed me out of my comfort zone and helped me to experience God in ways I wouldn't have otherwise had the opportunity to experience Him. My heart for giving and my faith in God have increased so much, simply because of being married to John and watching God at work in his life.

John would also tell you that, through our marriage, his eyes have been opened to the importance of evangelism and teaching. Within just a few weeks of our wedding day, he was by my side, going door-to-door on Saturday mornings, encouraging, praying, sharing the gospel, and ministering with me in an at-risk community our church had "adopted." Evangelism, telling people about Jesus, has always been an important part of my heart. And now, over a decade into marriage, it's part of John's too. He's stepped outside of his comfort zone time and time again and reached out to people in ways he might not have felt comfortable doing before. When you get married, you see the evidence of oneness played out in so many aspects of your life.

Anyone who goes into marriage believing they will remain the same will be gravely disappointed. The process of two becoming one in marriage is experienced in practical things, such as tastes and preferences, just as much as it is in the more significant things, like beliefs and character. Through marriage, you will most certainly transform along the way. You will grow, and change, and adapt. And the single most influential relationship in your life (outside of your relationship with God) is with the person you choose to marry. Because, for good or for bad, you will become "one" with whom you choose to unite (1 Corinthians 6:16). I can't stress this enough to all my single brothers and sisters: this is why it's so important to marry someone who will make you better.

## The Third Party

It's probably time for me to share a little secret with you: my husband loves someone else more than he loves me. To the outside listener, that might sound totally strange and maybe even completely inappropriate. You might think we're having marital problems or settling for a mediocre relationship. But for us, that thought makes complete sense in light of our personal relationship with God, through Jesus Christ.

My husband, John, loves God even more than he loves me. And I love God even more than I love my husband. It's always been that way, and my prayer is that it always will. Our individual relationship with God trumps our relationship with each other. And in my sincere opinion, that is the *very* truth that keeps our marriage alive, strong, and complete. For as many great days as we have in marriage, we also have days when we simply don't feel so great, days when one or both of us don't feel like loving, or giving, or forgiving. We feel hurt. We feel selfish. We may even feel that we've been wronged. In our humanity, we want to run, we want to hide, or we want to get revenge.

But in those moments, something *greater* takes over. Those are the very moments when our relationship with God becomes the anchor for our love, holding us in place. Our relationship with God is the supernatural relationship that pours into us so we can pour into each other. It allows us to continue growing as one and moving in the right direction. It holds us together.

## The Triangle

In my book *True Love Dates*, I spend some time talking about the Triangle Theory.[2] The Triangle Theory is a picture of our spiritual journey, and illustrates the idea that as two people move closer to God, they will inevitably move closer to each other as well.

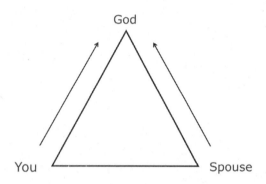

This applies to every relationship in our lives, but it especially applies to marriage. As Christians, we believe that when we enter into relationship with God, we're filled with His Spirit. It's the Spirit that breeds in us the qualities we need for a healthy life, and in turn, a healthy marriage. According to the Bible, the qualities of God's Spirit being poured out in a person's life are love, joy, peace, patience, kindness, goodness, faithfulness, gentleness, and self-control (Galatians 5:22-23). And as a professional counselor, I can tell you those are the *exact* qualities you need to have a thriving relationship. Is that simply a coincidence? I say no.

On the hard days, more than trusting my husband to love me like he should, I trust God's Spirit at work in his life. I am thankful that he loves God more than he loves me, because it's within his relationship with God that he's learned to love me like he should. And it's in my relationship with God that I've learned to love my husband like I should. Our relationship with God makes us better as individuals, and in turn, takes our relationship with each other to new heights. Because of God's transformational work in our lives, we become *better together*. Hands down, the best marriages I've witnessed are the ones displaying this kind of love, fueled by their unwavering commitment and devotion to Jesus Christ. It's a love that changes everything, slowly transforming both you and your spouse into the people God has called you to be.

But the triangle goes both ways, and just as you can take steps to move forward on your spiritual journey, sometimes you can find yourself stagnant, or even moving away. As John and I look back over the past decade of marriage, we realize the times when one or both of us struggled to stay connected to God were the times we also struggled the most to stay connected to each other.

One particularly hard season in our marriage was about five years ago. We were both making some extremely poor choices in how we were relating to each other and dealing with our stress. In hindsight, as we look back and try to take ownership of our choices and interactions, we can both openly admit that our walk with God was struggling as well. I was juggling my career and two little babies, all while walking through a serious episode of postpartum depression. John was in the thick of residency, working hours upon hours and facing some major stressors regarding the next steps of his career, all while trying to be there for (depressed) me and the kids. At a time when we both desperately needed God the most, we allowed our relationship with Him to take a backseat to the worries and stresses of life, and our marriage suffered for it. That year, some of the ugliest things inside of us began to surface and make their way into our marriage.

One night at 11:00 p.m., the result of all our poor choices came to a climax in one sweeping conversation that lasted well into the next morning. Something had to change, and it couldn't wait for tomorrow. It had to change *right now*.

We cried (oh did we cry), we confessed, we apologized, we prayed, and we committed to prioritizing God and each other in the most serious and deliberate way we knew how. You can be a Christian, committed to Jesus, and still take for granted how much He holds you together! As we look back, we know that was a defining year for us. We chose to move in God's direction by taking ownership of what needed to change and then committing to change. For us, there was no other option. And we haven't looked back since.

Over the past five years, the Lord has taken our marriage to heights of intimacy, love, passion, trust, and commitment we never imagined possible. And there's no doubt about it—this has been directly linked to our deepened intimacy with God. As we become "one" with God, He transforms us (1 Corinthians 6:17). And as He transforms us, we are empowered to become one with each other. Our relationship with God is the cord that holds us together, and "a cord of three strands is not quickly broken" (Ecclesiastes 4:12).

## Spiritual Intimacy

Not only does our relationship with God hold us together, but it unites us in a way that nothing else can do. When I travel across the country speaking to singles, I often talk about the power of spiritual boundaries in a dating relationship. Our culture tends to focus on physical and sexual boundaries, which are of much importance when you're single. But the power of spiritual intimacy can be even more intimate than a passionate kiss and more binding than sex. A deep connection occurs unlike anything else when two people are connecting on a spiritual level.

As I said in chapter 3, some of the most intimate moments I have with my husband are not "under the sheets" in our sexual relationship, but "over the sheets" as we sit hand in hand, baring our hearts and souls before the Lord, crying out together for our marriage, our family, and our world. Some of our best experiences revolve around the sharing of our hearts, inviting each other into the deepest places of who we are and the work God is doing within us. Spiritual intimacy occurs in our marriages when we don't just experience God at work in our lives, but we take the next step and share that journey with our spouse through mutual conversation, time together in prayer, serving with each other, and studying God's Word together.

To those of you who are single and reading this chapter, my prayer is that you will come away with a renewed perspective of what it means to marry someone who loves God more than they love you. If you are a believer and profess to have a relationship with Jesus Christ, there is no getting around the fact that your relationship with Jesus is by *far* the most influential relationship you will ever have. It's a relationship that will shape your identity, form your beliefs, influence your choices, and guide the entire purpose of your life. It's a relationship that, according to Scripture, will not just change you; it will *re-create* you. When you enter a relationship with Jesus, you're not simply a better version of yourself. You are completely made new (2 Corinthians 5:17).

Marrying a believer is not optional because through marriage, you are choosing to become *one* with another human being (2 Corinthians 6:14-17). You are joining your hearts, your minds, and your very bodies into an intimate and sacred connection. So many times I hear from men and women who try to "make it work" with someone who isn't in Christ. But there is no replacing the deep intimacy that comes when you are physically, emotionally, *and spiritually* connected to another human being. Nothing could *ever* replicate that experience. Don't sell yourself short out of fear and desperation, but instead, move toward God's promises in faith.

## Spiritual Disconnect

But what about you who are already in a marriage where there's a spiritual disconnect? What if you became a believer after you got married and find yourself in a marriage where you and your spouse are spiritually out of sync? Or what if you made the choice to marry someone who did not have a solid relationship with Jesus? A comment left by a young woman on one of my blog posts filled my heart with sadness. She wrote, "I was single until my mid 30s [when] I fell into temptation and now have a marriage relationship with an unbelieving man. It was so difficult being single and seeing my friends happy and paired off all before me, but not a day passes that I don't feel guilty and sad that I've for now lost my connection with the Lord. This is by far the most important thing in our lives—the Lord...all I can hope is that I can find my way back before it's too late."

I don't know the details of this woman's story, but I hear the discouragement and regret in her words. She expresses that she's strayed in her individual relationship with God and she wants to find her way back. Many of you are in the same boat. Maybe you've strayed in your relationship with Jesus, or maybe you're married to someone who is far from God—or someone who doesn't believe in God at all. What do you do when there is a spiritual disconnect between you and your spouse? According to God's Word, you simply do one thing: you commit. You commit to loving your spouse and being the best husband or wife you can be as far as it is up to you.

Let's look at the apostle Paul's advice about spiritual disconnect in marriage:

> If any brother has a wife who is not a believer and she is willing to live with him, he must not divorce her. And if a woman has a husband who is not a believer and he is willing to live with her, she must not divorce him. For the unbelieving husband has been sanctified through his wife, and the unbelieving wife has been sanctified through her believing husband. Otherwise your children would be unclean, but as it is, they are holy. But if the unbeliever leaves, let it be so. The brother or the sister is not bound in such circumstances; God has called us to live in peace. How do you know, wife, whether you will save your husband? Or, how do you know, husband, whether you will save your wife? (1 Corinthians 7:12-16).

The bottom line is this: as a believer, your connection with God has a profound influence over your spouse's life. When you become one through marriage, the God at work in your life is now part of the equation of the influence you have on your spouse's life. That doesn't guarantee that your spouse will one day choose to follow God, but it certainly gives you the affirmation that God has encouraged and empowered you to stay, to hope, to love, and to believe.

Recently a friend of mine shared a powerful story testifying to God's great work in her formerly unbelieving husband. When she got married she was young, and her personal relationship with God was at a weak point. Just like the woman who made a comment on my blog, she would say she had strayed from God. So when she got married, she didn't think much of the fact that her husband didn't claim to have a personal relationship with Jesus. But later in their marriage, specifically after having children, God began to do a work in her life. As her relationship with God was strengthened, it became more and more clear to her that she and her husband were not spiritually in sync, and it began to have a negative impact on their marriage.

She tried everything she knew to get him to deepen his personal faith and relationship with Jesus. But the more she talked, debated, and reasoned with him about her faith, the further he withdrew and shut down. So she decided to stop trying to change him, and instead chose to trust God with that process. She committed to prayer, and decided to become the best wife she knew how to be. She chose to honor him, to support him, and to love him even in their spiritual disconnect. And with time, the Lord began to do a great work in his life as well. God did what God does best: He calls, He saves, He redeems. My friend and her husband have come such a long way in their walk with Christ. They are both strong believers, secure in their relationship with Christ, and in turn, secure in their relationship with each other. Their story brings overwhelming joy to my heart, because it reminds me of the redemptive work of Christ possible in every single one of our lives.

If you find yourself struggling with spiritual disconnect in your marriage, I encourage you to commit to prayer. Cover your spouse in prayer from head to toe every day. And then, while you wait, commit to becoming the best spouse you can be. Hold on to hope, because your love and prayers alone are more effective than you could ever know. "Don't you wives realize that your husbands might be saved because of you? And don't you husbands realize that your wives might be saved because of you?" (1 Corinthians 7:16 NLT). Choose to honor, love, and respect your spouse in the best way you know how, and then trust God with the rest. Our prayers for the unbelieving spouse are so powerful, because God longs to draw people to His side. Because loving us is what He does best.

## Better Together

I asked some of my website readers to tell me their favorite thing about marriage. The most popular answer could be summed up in two words: *friendship* and *companionship*. There's something incredibly strengthening about the oneness of marriage. In marriage, you're given a lifelong partner, companion, helper, lover, and friend. Someone to confide in, to confess to, to cry with, to laugh with, and with whom you can experience the highs and lows of life. As God's Word says, we're better together!

> Two are better than one, because they have a good return for their labor: If either of them falls down, one can help the other up. But pity anyone who falls and has no one to help them up. Also, if two lie down together, they will keep warm. But how can one keep warm alone? Though one may be overpowered, two can defend themselves (Ecclesiastes 4:9-12).

According to this passage, two are better than one because they have a good return for their labor! They can do more together than they can do apart. With the love and support of a good spouse, there is no limit to what you can achieve in this world. But far and beyond achieving "life goals" is the incredible reward of pursuing spiritual goals—"kingdom goals." To be able to do more for God together than you could do apart is the ultimate achievement in marriage, and one that will last for eternity.

## More Than a Gift

Oneness in marriage is more than a gift we're given to enjoy; it's a responsibility entrusted to us. It's a call to become better together for the sake of one glorious thing: loving Christ and making Him known. The great mystery of marriage is that, in our oneness, we reflect the love of Christ to a lost and dying world. "'A man will leave his father and mother and be united to his wife, and the two will become one flesh.' This is a profound mystery—but I am talking about Christ and the church" (Ephesians 5:31-32). Oneness in marriage is a glimpse of the beautiful relationship we have with Christ, as sons and daughters of God (1 Corinthians 6:17).

In a world where marriages are falling apart all around us, we proclaim Christ's redemptive work in our lives every time we choose *we* over *me*. When marital oneness is lived out, we give the world a glimpse of a love and union that transcends this world, because it comes from above, from a God who overcame sin and death just to be *united* with us. Oh, oneness is a great gift, but it's an even greater responsibility. A responsibility to reflect the love of God to a lost and dying world. May God give us the strength we need to accept this great gift and the determination to model it to the world around us.

# REFLECTION QUESTIONS
# FOR MARRIED COUPLES

1. On the scale of codependence—interdependence—total independence, which category do you tend to exhibit the most in your marriage? What steps can you take toward achieving a heightened sense of interdependence in your marriage?

2. In what ways has the process of oneness made you more like your spouse and vice versa? Take some time to discuss some positive ways you've influenced each other through your marriage.

3. Would you describe your marriage as spiritually connected or spiritually disconnected? If the first, what are some ways you can strengthen your individual relationship with God as you move "up" the triangle? What are some ways you can continue strengthening your spiritual connection with each other?

   If the second, what are some ways you can strengthen your individual relationship with God? In what ways can you commit to praying for your spouse this week? What is one tangible action you can take to be the best spouse you can be?

## REFLECTION QUESTIONS
## FOR SINGLES

1. On the scale of codependence—interdependence—total independence, which category do you tend to exhibit in your personal relationships? Have any of your past relationships been based on "need"? Give some examples.

2. What are some factors that may have influenced how you engage in interpersonal relationships? What are some steps you can take toward "filling yourself up" and achieving healthy interdependence?

3. In this chapter we discussed the importance of spiritual oneness and the idea of marrying someone who loves God more than they love you. Have your past dating relationships reflected this as a priority? Why or why not?

4. How can you apply the Triangle Theory to your current relationship status (whether you are single or dating)? What are some ways you can strengthen your individual relationship with God and move toward His direction?

10

# The Beautiful Exchange

*From Me to We*

My name changed the moment I first met John. And I'm not talking about my last name (though that also changed a few days after we got married). I'm talking about my first name. My birth name is Debra, but my nickname had always been Debbie. That's what everyone called me. My parents, my family, and all my friends at school. To the little part of the world that knew me, I was Debbie. My identity was wrapped up in that six-letter name.

Now fast-forward a couple of decades to when I met John Fileta at a conference in Boston for the very first time. It was the Fourth of July weekend, and after noticing each other from across the room, our paths finally crossed and we introduced ourselves. I'm not sure why it happened, but even though I introduced myself to him as Debbie, for some reason he just started calling me Deb. I don't know if he misheard me, or if he just decided to go ahead and shorten my name, but whatever the reason, he referred to me as Deb from that moment forward.

Any of you Debras out there *know* there is a huge difference between a Debbie and a Deb. Debbies are cute, funny, and sweet.

Debs are serious, to the point, and brash. Debbies are charming and the life of a party. Debs are blunt and a little rough around the edges. Everyone wants to be a Debbie. No one wants to be a Deb. I know I sure didn't. But after a few weeks of John calling me Deb, I started to find it endearing. I mean, no one else in the world called me Deb but him. It was sort of like his special name for me. So I decided not to correct him. Months later, after we started dating, I found myself identifying with the name Deb. It was almost like adding a new piece to the puzzle of my life and identity. I eventually started introducing myself as Deb when I was with him. I was his Deb, and I liked it.

Now the name has stuck. The funny thing is, you can tell precisely how someone knows me just by listening to what they call me. It's almost like a timeline of my life. If they call me Debbie, there's a good chance they are a relative or someone I know from childhood, high school, or college. If they call me Debra, it's likely someone who knows me from my career or professional world. But if they call me Deb, you can guarantee they met me during my P.J. years (post John). You might say I lost my childhood nickname, but you could also say I gained a special new nickname.

## Losing Your Self

This story is a funny little glimpse into my personal life, but more than that, it's an important analogy into the exchange that occurs within the context of a marriage. Marriage is the *hardest* and *greatest* thing you'll ever do, because through marriage you are called to "lose your self" to gain so much more. When you hear the term "lose your self," you might rebel against that idea, and rightly so. I, for one, am a huge advocate for people not losing themselves in a dating relationship, but rather, committing to finding themselves long before they get married. They should dedicate the time and energy it takes to get to know themselves first and to get to know themselves well. To attract and sustain a healthy marriage, singles should become as healthy and whole as they can while standing alone and remain that way through marriage. I dedicated my entire first book to this important concept.

But in the formula of marriage, I'm talking about a different kind of "loss." I'm not talking about the loss of identity, but about the loss of self. They might sound like the same thing, but they are completely different. The loss of self has nothing to do with losing our identity or our personality. It doesn't mean we ignore our needs, wants, and desires or let go of our goals and dreams. No, letting go of self means one thing and one thing alone: we choose to lose all that is wrong in exchange for all that is right. Losing our "selves" means we let go of all that God has called us *not to be* in exchange for all He has called us *to be*. Through every season of marriage, we're invited to take part in this beautiful exchange time and time again, becoming better and better along the way.

## The Four Seasons of Marriage

Every marriage goes through its seasons of ups and its seasons of downs. Along the journey of marriage, there are incredible times, unforgettable memories, and intimate experiences, but also times of stress, moments of hurt, and even seasons of grief. While every marriage travels its own unique journey, through my years of relationship counseling I've observed that just like in nature, every relationship passes through similar seasons.

In *True Love Dates*, I refer to these as the "Four Seasons of Dating," but the same concepts and principles are also observed within the context of marriage, just in a different way and for a different purpose. If the seasons of dating expose the character of the person we're dating, the seasons of marriage expose our own character, revealing what we need to change and the areas we need to develop. Every stage of marriage offers us an opportunity to learn, to grow, and to transform. Every season invites us into the beautiful exchange of our weaknesses, in return for God's strength (2 Corinthians 12:10).

## Spring

Spring is the season of new beginnings in marriage. In spring, emotions run high and passion is plentiful. Many marriage experts refer to these first few years of marriage as the "honeymoon stage" because that's typically when stress is low and attraction is high. It's the start of life together. For many newlyweds, spring is the time when they are learning more about each other than they ever learned before as they unite their lives into one. It's a season with little distractions and the ability to focus on each other in a deliberate and meaningful way. Whether it lasts a few weeks, a few months, or a few years, spring is a beautiful time of marriage, which is why many couples tend to get anxious when the bliss of spring begins to fade into the heat of summer.

## Summer

Summer is the season when "things get hot." The heat of life is burning bright with its worries and struggles. From financial stress, to family stress. From physical concerns, all the way to sexual concerns. From the strain of work and caring for children, to the reality of managing a home and the tasks of daily life. The heat is everywhere. And the hotter it gets, the more layers you start to shed, revealing who you really are deep down. It is said that hardships don't create your character; rather, they reveal your character. There is no greater opportunity for your true character to be revealed than through the season of summer. This season of marriage forces you to come to terms with the facade you bring into marriage and invites you to live authentically.

In summer, you realize there is no place to hide within the day-in-day-out interactions of marriage. Your habits, emotional temperament, personality, and quirks are all exposed to the person before you. In summer, a married couple often finds they're beginning to shed the *expectations* they had of marriage in exchange for the *reality* of what marriage is truly like. Through the heat of the pressure cooker of marriage, you begin learning things about your spouse and seeing things in yourself you never knew existed, things you may not have recognized or experienced through dating. You see your selfishness, your pride, your sins, and your struggles in a whole new light. And as layers are shed and the facade begins to come down, you also see your spouse's weaknesses more than ever before as they are intensified through the magnifying glass of marriage.

In summer, you come to the difficult realization that you can burn your spouse as quickly as you can get burned by them. You and your spouse can hurt each other in ways you never thought possible. And as the wear and tear of life and children and stress begin to take their toll, you find that the heat of summer can either move your marriage into the heat of irreplaceable commitment and deepened intimacy or the heat of deepened pain.

## Fall

Fall is the season of marriage when your true colors are shining brightly. By fall, you know more about your spouse than you ever thought you could know. You know every quirk, every strength, every weakness. You know what gets them excited, as well as every button you could possibly push to drive them mad. And because of that, fall is the season of marriage that tends to be laced with the most potential for both *conflict* and *communication*. If passion carried you through spring, and emotions carried you through summer, then communication is what will carry you through fall.

In fall, you're given the regular opportunity to handle disagreement in a way that will either make you better or make you bitter. You're exposed to your communication style, and you must choose between being passive, aggressive, or respectfully assertive. You must navigate through the many "walls" that tend to prevent healthy communication and choose to bring them down as you move toward your spouse each day. And as you journey through the problem spots of fall, you find that you're either moving forward and making progress or getting stuck in the same ruts over and over again. The conflict of fall can be the catalyst that draws you together and deepens your roots, or slowly your leaves begin to wither away.

## Winter

Out of all the seasons of marriage, winter can be the hardest. Many couples find themselves trekking through the frozen tundra of winter, a long, cold season with seemingly no end in sight. They feel tired, they feel drained, they feel apathetic, and maybe they feel as though their affections toward each other have cooled to a place beyond resuscitation. The passion they once had feels like a faint memory. The emotion that fueled them feels like it has run dry. The fire between them has frozen over, and they wonder if this is the end.

For those of you who might be walking through the season of winter, let me remind you that *winter is not the end of the road.* Emotions may have cooled, and passion may have dwindled, but only for a season. While this may be a time of hibernation, it is also a time of strengthening and preparation. It's a time of refueling our energy and recalibrating our hearts to the slow and steady hope of healing. It's the opportunity to choose the actions of love, even when the feelings of love might be lingering far behind. Winter is by far the greatest opportunity to choose marriage, remembering that it is only by pushing through the hard things that we get to take joy in the remarkable things to come. Winter is not the end of the road, dear friends. In fact, maybe it's only the beginning.

## Spring Again

As with the seasons of nature, the seasons of marriage tend to come and go. Just as subtly as it began, one season fades into another. For you who are struggling through a particularly difficult season, know that many couples who experienced winter found the season of spring was just around the corner once again. And often it's even better and more fulfilling than they ever imagined it could be. I know of so many couples living through the "golden years" of their marriage who report that the joy, passion, and connection they feel in the spring after 50 years of marriage is even more alive than the spring they felt as newlyweds.

Research affirms these reports in finding that there is a tendency for marital satisfaction to increase in the later stages of marriage, specifically during the middle-age and empty-nest phase.[1] One study found married couples to be happier after 40 years of marriage than they were in any other stage or season of marriage, including the honeymoon stage.[2] What a fascinating observation, and one that totally obliterates the false expectation society tends to portray that marriage gets "worse" with each passing year.

> Each season of marriage takes you deeper.

Hope is up ahead because each season of marriage takes you deeper. Each season grows your love. Each season strengthens your commitment. But hear me on this: it's not the season itself that will make or break your marriage; it's what you choose to do within that season. In every season we're given the opportunity to mature, to heal, to grow, to learn, and to change. We're given the chance to let go of our sin, our weakness, our pride, and our selfishness in exchange for something greater. We're given the choice to love, to honor, to serve, and to lay down our lives. Time and time again, we're asked to choose marriage. And in those daily choices we find that, in choosing marriage, we're also choosing to become better along the way.

### Brad and Kate's Story

When I met Brad and Kate at the church we attend, the first thing I noticed about them was their passion for marriage and their passion for each other. They lead a marriage ministry at our church and write a marriage blog to encourage other couples, and it's clear to everyone that they love being married. But believe it or not, it wasn't always that way. There was a time when Brad and Kate had to walk through their own journey of marital hardships, a time when they wondered whether their marriage would come out the other side.

Brad and Kate started as high school sweethearts who couldn't wait for the day when they could commit to each other in marriage. When the day finally arrived, they believed their love for each other and their love for the Lord would carry them through any hardships life could bring their way. But about six months into their marriage, the reality of becoming one hit them like a ton of bricks. The warm and passionate season of spring quickly moved into the heat and struggle of summer. Kate describes it like this: "The reality of marriage was like a slap in the face to the dream we had built up in our hearts and in our minds."

For this young couple, the very thing they had waited and looked forward to in marriage became the very thing that brought the most struggle. "As a woman who had deeply desired sex with her future husband," Kate says, "about six months into marriage I found myself struggling with desire. I loved my husband deeply, found him desirable and yet didn't desire sex. It didn't take long for me to feel isolated and alone. Sex was a topic that wasn't talked about in church and wasn't safe enough for me to ask for help from those around me. I hurt and struggled in silence with Brad feeling vast amounts of frustration and hurt as well."

Brad also reflects on that time in their life. "As a new husband I was thrilled to enjoy sex with my wife. But I forgot that was not the only part of becoming one. I was consumed in my own selfish desires. I would regularly put my needs, my time, and my desires above my wife's. This left her feeling abandoned and alone. I put the blame for that lack of connection squarely on her lack of a desire for sex. Meanwhile, I couldn't see through my own cloud to understand the need for deeper intimacy to accompany sexual intimacy." For Brad and

Kate, it was the expectations for their sex life meeting the reality of their sexual struggles that brought them from the heat of summer into the conflict of fall. Unequipped to communicate and ill-prepared to handle this conflict, they quickly found themselves in the emotional frost of winter. "Sadly," says Kate, "we stayed in the season of winter for quite some time until the thaw started and the hope of Jesus that never changes sprang new life from our desolate battlefield."

Winter was not the end of their story. The thaw began when each of them decided they would make it a priority to stop looking for the other to change, and instead begin to make change in themselves. Kate summed it up best when she said, "I began to change *me* one thing at a time with a lot of prayer and God's Word, and the thaw began." The first step to changing your marriage is to begin changing yourself. Change is contagious, and eventually the change in their individual lives began to fuel the change in their relationship. And in time, the thaw of winter led them to spring once again.

Today, Brad and Kate are happily married and both serving on staff at our church in roles that bring hope and offer encouragement to couples who might be going through the hardships of marriage. Their story is just one of the many stories I hear of redemption, and proof that even after a particularly hard season of marriage, God can restore, redeem, and reignite. In every marriage a couple will go through their own unique set of struggles when their expectations of marriage come face-to-face with the reality of marriage. But after the spring of passion subsides, the heat of summer rises, the conflict of fall fades, and the chill of winter passes, there is always hope that the joy of spring will come again.

## Laying It All Down

Nothing can move us into the beautiful exchange of marriage more than the knowledge of the greatest exchange that took place for every one of us. In this beautiful exchange, the greatest one of all,

Jesus Christ exchanged His life to redeem our weaknesses, our brokenness, our sins, and our struggles. In this beautiful exchange, He took upon Himself all that He is *not* to free us to become all that He has called us to be. All for love, He sacrificed the greatest thing of all: His very life. "This is how we know what love is: Jesus Christ laid down his life for us. And we ought to lay down our lives for our brothers and sisters" (1 John 3:16). Because of this exchange, we can know love. Because of this exchange, we are freed to give love. There is no greater love than the laying down of one's own life for another (John 15:13). And in marriage, we're called to daily lay it all down for the sake of another. We're called to love, to give, and to forgive like we've never done before.

And just as Christ rose again, so we can rise again too. After the struggle of death, there will always come the victory of life (Romans 6:11). Those who know Christ in the suffering of His death will also know Him in the power of His resurrection (Philippians 3:10-11). No matter what hardship you are facing today, be encouraged that, through Christ, there is hope of resurrection. There is hope of reconciliation. There is hope of redemption.

## The Beautiful Exchange

Those who know me well know I'm a realist at heart. I don't like to beat around the bush. I prefer to respectfully and affirmingly "say it like it is." I've often been described as compassionate yet candid in both my counseling and my writing style. If you've read any of my articles, you know I'm not a fan of romanticizing marriage and relationships. I'd rather encourage people to have accurate expectations and healthy interactions. Which is why, when I felt led to write this book, I originally wanted to call it *Marriage Will Cost You*. I know, I know. It sounds intense. And my guess was that title probably wasn't going to go over well with my marketing team.

But as I began to pray and think through this project, I realized that while marriage is certainly "costly," *the cost of marriage* is not the end of the story. It's nowhere near the end. Describing this project as the cost of marriage doesn't do it justice, because when the focus is simply on the cost, we miss something of ultimate value: the incredible gain.

Everything of value—and that is exactly what marriage is, a most valuable and cherished possession—is costly. Scripture affirms this value and refers to finding a good spouse as though they are a precious gem or a royal crown (Proverbs 31:10; 12:4). The analogy portrays the sheer blessing of finding someone who adds value to your life. Marriage isn't just about the sacrificial cost; it's about so much more. It's about the great gain. It's about the beautiful exchange that occurs in our lives when we let go of the wrong in exchange for what is right. And ultimately, what we give is nothing compared to what we end up receiving.

We're invited to exchange our selfishness for holiness.

Our vulnerability for intimacy.

Our pride for humility.

Our assumptions for truth.

Our insecurities for safety.

Our facade for authenticity.

Our infatuation for adoration.

Our independence for oneness.

All that we are not, for all that God calls us to be.

While that exchange is certainly costly, it pales in comparison to the great reward we receive in the end: less of us, and more of Him. "He must become greater; I must become less" (John 3:30). The emptier we feel, the more He can fill us. The less we have, the more we can receive. The weaker we are, the stronger Christ makes us. The more we give, the better we become. It's the irony of the beautiful exchange that will occur time and time again in our lives and in our marriages, if only we invite it to change us. If only we allow it to refine us.

My prayer for me, and for every one of you reading this book, is that we would be encouraged and empowered to daily let go of self and step into everything God has called us to be. No matter what your relationship status, whether single or married or somewhere in between, may you allow God to use the relationships He's placed in your life as an opportunity to enter into the beautiful exchange—the exchange that will replace more of us with more of Him. And as we do, may we watch the transformation within us begin to influence those around us.

Often in life, the *hardest* things we're called to do are also the *greatest*. Choosing marriage is certainly one of those things. May God give us the strength we need to choose the hard things, the grace we need to receive the great things, and the perseverance to become better each step of the way.

> Now to him who is able to do immeasurably more than all we ask or imagine, according to his power that is at work within us, to him be glory in the church and in Christ Jesus throughout all generations, for ever and ever! Amen (Ephesians 3:20-21).

# REFLECTION QUESTIONS
## FOR MARRIED COUPLES

1. Reviewing the four seasons of marriage, which season(s) do you find yourself currently in? What are some of the things you are experiencing as a couple or as individuals within this season?

2. Reflect on the years you've been married and discuss the times you found yourself in the season of spring. What are the actions, behaviors, and interactions that foster the season of spring in your marriage? What needs to happen to enter spring again?

3. Read 1 John 3:16 together. What does it mean to lay down our lives in marriage? What actions, behaviors, and interactions reflect that kind of love on a day-to-day basis?

4. Marriage is about the beautiful exchange that occurs when we let go of the wrong in exchange for what is right. Discuss some negative traits or behaviors that have been exchanged for something better in your marriage (example: pride for humility).

5. The first step to changing your marriage is to begin changing yourself. Reflecting on the chapters in this book, what steps are you going to take toward change in yourself and in your marriage?

# REFLECTION QUESTIONS
# FOR SINGLES

1. In the beginning of this chapter, I referred to the importance of not losing your identity in a relationship. In what ways are you understanding, creating, and living out your true identity in this stage of life?

2. Think back on a marriage you witnessed of someone close to you or from your family of origin. What seasons of marriage did you watch them go through, and were those seasons navigated in a healthy or unhealthy way?

3. The beautiful exchange occurs in any relationship where we allow God to refine us through the process of interacting with others, making us more like Christ. Write down the names of a few friends you have invited into your life to foster growth and change. If you can't think of anyone, how can you take steps to build those types of friendships in your life?

4. Reflect on John 3:30. What steps can you take to allow Christ to become greater in your life as you become less? What relationships, habits, interactions, or behaviors do you need to let go of to make room for the "beautiful exchange"?

# Acknowledgments

The process of writing this book has been more about listening than teaching. It has been an intimate time of connecting with God, asking Him to transform my heart, to refine my character, and to enrich my marriage. He's met me in ways that have built my faith and deepened my affection for Him and the work He's called me to do. I don't know why He's chosen me to deliver this message, but I'm humbled and completely aware that it's not my message and it has never been. *Everything I do, I do for You, Jesus. Thank You for entrusting me with this message and teaching me with these words. Do with them whatever You see fit.*

I'm so grateful for my husband, John, the incredible man God knew I needed. He has been my strong partner, my safe place, my best friend, and my biggest fan throughout this entire process— but more importantly, throughout life. Growing, learning, and maturing with him by my side through the last decade of our marriage has been my greatest honor and privilege. The highs and lows we've been through have deepened our love, strengthened our commitment, and reminded us that together with Christ, there's nothing we can't overcome. *I love you more than words can express. "Go with me, my love."*

To my beautiful children, incredible family, committed friends, faithful readers, loyal literary agency, talented publishing team, passionate ministry leaders, and everyone else who has had a hand in the process of taking an idea and turning it into a message—I'm so grateful. Let's continue to trust God with the seeds we've sown for His glory.

# Notes

## A Note from the Author

1. William Nicholson, screenwriter, *Shadowlands,* Price Entertainment, 1993.

## Chapter 1—Choosing Marriage

1. "2016 Average Cost of Wedding in the U.S. up 3/10ths of a Percent to $26,720," *The Wedding Report,* accessed August 22, 2017, www.theweddingreport.com/index.cfm/action/blog/view/post/pid/660/title/2016.

2. Tim Henderson, "For Many Millennials, Marriage Can Wait," The Pew Charitable Trusts, December 20, 2016, http://www.pewtrusts.org/en/research-and-analysis/blogs/stateline/2016/12/20/for-many-millennials-marriage-can-wait.

3. Anthony D'Ambrosio, "5 Reasons Marriage Doesn't Work Anymore," WCNC, February 8, 2017, http://www.wcnc.com/opinion/5-reasons-we-cant-handle-marriage-anymore/213234475.

4. D'Ambrosio, "5 Reasons Marriage Doesn't Work Anymore."

5. Timothy J. Keller, *The Meaning of Marriage* (New York: Penguin Books, 2013), 90.

6. Louis de Bernières, *Corelli's Mandolin* (New York: Vintage International, 1994), 281.

## Chapter 2—We > Me

1. Sheldon Vanauken, *A Severe Mercy* (HarperSanFrancisco, 1980), 39.

## Chapter 3—Walls Will Fall

1. "Great Wall of China," History.com, July 12, 2017, http://www.history.com/topics/great-wall-of-china.

2. "Great Wall of China," History.com.

3. George E. Vaillant, *Ego Mechanisms of Defense: A Guide for Clinicians and Researchers* (Washington, DC: American Psychiatric Publishing, 1992), 3-4.

4. H.J. Markman, S.M. Stanley, and S.L. Blumberg, *Fighting for Your Marriage* (San Francisco: Jossey-Bass, 2010), 2.

5. Markman, Stanley, and Blumberg, *Fighting for Your Marriage*, 11.

6. J.M. Gottman and R.W. Levenson, "A Two-Factor Model of Predicting When a Couple Will Divorce; Exploratory Analysis Using 14-Year Longitudinal Data," *Family Processes Journal* 41, no. 1 (2002), 83-96, https://www.gottman.com/about/research/couples.

7. American Psychological Association, http://www.apa.org/topics/divorce/.

8. Markman, Stanley, and Blumberg, *Fighting for Your Marriage*, 112.

9. Ibid

## Chapter 4—Alter That Ego

1. *The Diagnostic and Statistical Manual of Mental Disorders, Fifth Edition, DSM-V* (Washington, DC: American Psychological Association, 2013), 669-70.

2. *The Diagnostic and Statistical Manual of Mental Disorders, Fifth Edition, DSM-V*, 671.

3. Walter Dunnett, "Pride," *Bible Study Tools*, July 13, 2017, http://www.biblestudytools.com/dictionary/pride/.

4. Robert Robinson, "Come Thou Fount of Every Blessing," 1757.

5. Jennifer E. Farrell, et al., "Humility and Relationship Outcomes in Couples: The Mediating Role of Commitment," *Couple and Family Psychology: Research and Practice* 4, no. 1 (2015): 14-26, doi: 10.1037/cfp0000033.

## Chapter 6—Always Use Protection

1. Henry Cloud and John Townsend, *Boundaries* (Grand Rapids, MI: Zondervan, 1992).

2. Heather Bryce, "After the Affair: A Wife's Story," *Christianity Today,* Winter 1988, http://www.christianitytoday.com/pastors/1988/winter/88l1058.html.

3. Cheryl Chumley, "Facebook Cited in a Third of All Divorce Cases," *The Washington Times*, January 21, 2015, http://www.washingtontimes.com/news/2015/jan/21/facebook-cited-in-a-third-of-all-divorce-cases-its/.

4. Jarrid Wilson, "Why I'm Getting a Divorce in 2014," JarridWilson.com, December 31, 2013, http://jarridwilson.com/why-im-getting-a-divorce-in-2014.

## Chapter 7—#RealTalk

1. Kate Fagan, "Split Image," Espn.com, May 7, 2015, http://www.espn.com/espn/feature/story/_/id/12833146/instagram-account-university-pennsylvania-runner-showed-only-part-story.

2. Timothy J. Keller, *The Meaning of Marriage* (New York: Penguin Books, 2013), 101.

3. "Hillsong Pastor Michael Guglielmucci on Today Tonight," August 27, 2008, https://www.youtube.com/watch?v=HcswYwQczPc.

4. Jeffrey Dew, Sonya Britt, and Sandra Huston, "Examining the Relationship Between Financial Issues and Divorce," *Family Relations Journal* 61, no. 4 (Sept. 2012): doi: 10.1111/j.1741-3729.2012.00715.x.

## Chapter 8—Sex Marks the Spot

1. Cavan Sieczkowski, "Man Sends Wife Spreadsheet of All Her Excuses Not to Have Sex," *The Huffington Post*, July 21, 2014, http://www.huffingtonpost.com/2014/07/21/man-wife-spreadsheet-sex_n_5605670.html.

2. Roy F. Baumeister, Kathleen R. Catanese, and Kathleen D. Vohs, "Is There a Gender Difference in Strength of Sex Drive? Theoretical Views, Conceptual Distinctions, and a Review of Relevant Evidence," *Personality and Social Psychology Review* 5, no. 3 (Aug. 2001): 242-73, doi: 10.1207/S15327957PSPR0503_5.

3. Kevin Leman, *Sheet Music: Uncovering the Secrets of Sexual Intimacy in Marriage* (Carol Stream, IL: Tyndale House, 2003), 255-56.

4. Anne Ortlund, *Disciplines of the Beautiful Woman* (Nashville, TN: W Publishing Group, 1984), 48.

5. Johnathon Bowers, "America's Most Tolerated Sin," *DesiringGod.org*, February 18, 2015, http://www.desiringgod.org/messages/america-s-most-tolerated-sin.

6. Colette Bouchez, "Better Sex: What's Weight Got to Do With It?", WebMD, http://www.webmd.com/sex-relationships/features/sex-and-weight#1.

7. Gary Thomas, *Cherish* (Grand Rapids, MI: Zondervan, 2017), 31.

## Chapter 9—Better Together

1. *The Diagnostic and Statistical Manual of Mental Disorders, Fifth Edition, DSM-V* (Washington, DC: American Psychological Association, 2013), 675.

2. Debra Fileta, *True Love Dates* (Grand Rapids, MI: Zondervan, 2013), 126.

## Chapter 10—The Beautiful Exchange

1. Gorchoff S.M., John O.P., Helson R., "Contextualizing Change in Marital Satisfaction During Middle Age: An 18-Year Longitudinal Study," *Psychological Science* 19, no. 11 (Nov. 2008): doi: 10.1111/j.1467-9280.2008.02222.x.

2. "First Year of Marriage Unhappiest," December 3, 2012, http://www.deakin.edu.au/about-deakin/media-releases/articles/2012/first-year-of-marriage-unhappiest.

# About the Author

**Debra Fileta** is a licensed professional counselor, national speaker, relationship expert, and author of the book *True Love Dates: Your Indispensable Guide to Finding the Love of Your Life*. She's the creator of the popular relationship blog, TrueLoveDates.com, where she writes candidly about love, sex, marriage, and dating. Her blog offers hundreds of articles, courses, and resources and reaches millions of people every year with the message that healthy people make healthy relationships. You may recognize her voice from her 200+ articles in magazines and publications such as *Relevant Magazine, Crosswalk. com, IAmSecond, Boundless, Christianity Today*, and many more across the web.

She and her husband, John, have been joyfully *choosing marriage* for more than a decade and have three beautiful children. As an extrovert, she loves interacting with her readers, so take a minute to connect with her on Facebook (www.facebook.com/TrueLoveDates) and Twitter (@DebFileta) or reach out to her at debra@truelovedates.com.